A Collection of Stor

by Jack London

Contents:

The Human Drift Small-Boat Sailing Four Horses and a Sailor Nothing that Ever Came to Anything That Dead Men Rise up Never A Classic of the Sea A Wicked Woman (Curtain Raiser) The Birth Mark (Sketch)

THE HUMAN DRIFT

"The Revelations of Devout and Learn'd Who rose before us, and as Prophets Burn'd, Are all but stories, which, awoke from Sleep, They told their comrades, and to Sleep return'd."

The history of civilisation is a history of wandering, sword in hand, in search of food. In the misty younger world we catch glimpses of phantom races, rising, slaying, finding food, building rude civilisations, decaying, falling under the swords of stronger hands, and passing utterly away. Man, like any other animal, has roved over the earth seeking what he might devour; and not romance and adventure, but the hunger-need, has urged him on his vast adventures. Whether a bankrupt gentleman sailing to colonise Virginia or a lean Cantonese contracting to labour on the sugar plantations of Hawaii, in each case, gentleman and coolie, it is a desperate attempt to get something to eat, to get more to eat than he can get at home.

It has always been so, from the time of the first pre-human anthropoid crossing a mountain-divide in quest of better berry-bushes beyond, down to the latest Slovak, arriving on our shores to-day, to go to work in the coal-mines of Pennsylvania. These migratory movements of peoples have been called drifts, and the word is apposite. Unplanned, blind, automatic, spurred on by the pain of hunger, man has literally drifted his way around the planet. There have been drifts in the past, innumerable and forgotten, and so remote that no records have been left, or composed of such low-typed humans or pre-humans that they made no scratchings on stone or bone and left no monuments to show that they had been.

These early drifts we conjecture and know must have occurred, just as we know that the first upright-walking brutes were descended from some kin of the quadrumana through having developed "a pair of great toes out of two opposable thumbs." Dominated by fear, and by their very fear accelerating their development, these early ancestors of ours, suffering hunger-pangs very like the ones we experience to-day, drifted on, hunting and being hunted, eating and being eaten, wandering through thousand-year- long odysseys of screaming primordial savagery, until they left their skeletons in glacial gravels, some of them, and their bone-scratchings in cave-men's lairs.

There have been drifts from east to west and west to east, from north to south and back again, drifts that have criss-crossed one another, and drifts colliding and recoiling and caroming off in new directions. From Central Europe the Aryans have drifted into Asia, and from Central Asia the Turanians have drifted across Europe. Asia has thrown forth great waves of hungry humans from the prehistoric "round-barrow" "broad-heads" who overran Europe and penetrated to Scandinavia and England, down through the hordes of Attila and Tamerlane, to the present immigration of Chinese and Japanese that threatens America. The Phoenicians and the Greeks, with unremembered drifts behind them, colonised the Mediterranean. Rome was engulfed in the torrent of Germanic tribes drifting down from the north before a flood of drifting Asiatics. The Angles, Saxons, and Jutes, after having drifted whence no man knows, poured into Britain, and the English have carried this drift on around the world. Retreating before stronger breeds, hungry and voracious, the Eskimo has drifted to the inhospitable polar regions, the Pigmy to the fever-rotten jungles of Africa. And in this day the drift of the races continues, whether it be of Chinese into the Philippines and the Malay Peninsula, of Europeans to the United States or of Americans to the wheat- lands of Manitoba and the Northwest.

Perhaps most amazing has been the South Sea Drift. Blind, fortuitous, precarious as no other drift has been, nevertheless the islands in that waste of ocean have received drift after drift of the races. Down from the mainland of Asia poured an Aryan drift that built civilisations in Ceylon, Java, and Sumatra.

Only the monuments of these Aryans remain. They themselves have perished utterly, though not until after leaving evidences of their drift clear across the great South Pacific to far Easter Island. And on that drift they encountered races who had accomplished the drift before them, and they, the Aryans, passed, in turn, before the drift of other and subsequent races whom we to-day call the Polynesian and the Melanesian.

Man early discovered death. As soon as his evolution permitted, he made himself better devices for killing than the old natural ones of fang and claw. He devoted himself to the invention of killing devices before he discovered fire or manufactured for himself religion. And to this day, his finest creative energy and technical skill are devoted to the same old task of making better and ever better killing weapons. All his days, down all the past, have been spent in killing. And from the fear-stricken, jungle-lurking, cave-haunting creature of long ago, he won to empery over the whole animal world because he developed into the most terrible and awful killer of all the animals. He found himself crowded. He killed to make room, and as he made room ever he increased and found himself crowded, and ever he went on killing to make more room. Like a settler clearing land of its weeds and forest bushes in order to plant corn, so man was compelled to clear all manner of life away in order to plant himself. And, sword in hand, he has literally hewn his way through the vast masses of life that occupied the earth space he coveted for himself. And ever he has carried the battle wider and wider, until to-day not only is he a far more capable killer of men and animals than ever before, but he has pressed the battle home to the infinite and invisible hosts of menacing lives in the world of micro-organisms.

It is true, that they that rose by the sword perished by the sword. And yet, not only did they not all perish, but more rose by the sword than perished by it, else man would not to-day be over-running the world in such huge swarms. Also, it must not be forgotten that they who did not rise by the sword did not rise at all. They were not. In view of this, there is something wrong with Doctor Jordan's war-theory, which is to the effect that the best being sent out to war, only the second best, the men who are left, remain to breed a second-best race, and that, therefore, the human race deteriorates under war. If this be so, if we have sent forth the best we bred and gone on breeding from the men who were left, and since we have done this for ten thousand millenniums and are what we splendidly are to-day, then what unthinkably splendid and god-like beings must have been our forebears those ten thousand millenniums ago! Unfortunately for Doctor Jordan's theory, those ancient forebears cannot live up to this fine reputation. We know them for what they were, and before the monkey cage of any menagerie we catch truer glimpses and hints and resemblances of what our ancestors really were long and long ago. And by killing, incessant killing, by making a shambles of the planet, those ape-like creatures have developed even into you and me. As Henley has said in "The Song of the Sword":

"The Sword Singing--

Driving the darkness, Even as the banners And spear of the Morning; Sifting the nations, The Slag from the metal, The waste and the weak From the fit and the strong; Fighting the brute, The abysmal Fecundity; Checking the gross Multitudinous blunders, The groping, the purblind Excesses in service Of the Womb universal, The absolute drudge."

As time passed and man increased, he drifted ever farther afield in search of room. He encountered other drifts of men, and the killing of men became prodigious. The weak and the decadent fell under the sword. Nations that faltered, that waxed prosperous in fat valleys and rich river deltas, were swept away by the drifts of stronger men who were nourished on the hardships of deserts and mountains and who were more capable with the sword. Unknown and unnumbered billions of men have been so destroyed in prehistoric times. Draper says that in the twenty years of the Gothic war, Italy lost 15,000,000 of her population; "and that the wars, famines, and pestilences of the reign of Justinian diminished the human species by the almost incredible number of 100,000,000." Germany, in the Thirty Years' War, lost 6,000,000 inhabitants. The record of our own American Civil War need scarcely be recalled.

And man has been destroyed in other ways than by the sword. Flood, famine, pestilence and murder are potent factors in reducing population--in making room. As Mr. Charles Woodruff, in his "Expansion of Races," has instanced: In 1886, when the dikes of the Yellow River burst, 7,000,000 people were drowned. The failure of crops in Ireland, in 1848, caused 1,000,000 deaths. The famines in India of 1896-7 and 1899-1900 lessened the population by 21,000,000. The T'ai'ping rebellion and the Mohammedan rebellion, combined with the famine of 1877-78, destroyed scores of millions of Chinese. Europe has been swept repeatedly by great plagues. In India, for the period of 1903 to 1907, the plague deaths averaged between one and two millions a year. Mr. Woodruff is responsible for the assertion that 10,000,000 persons now living in the United States are doomed to die of tuberculosis. And in this same country ten thousand persons a year are directly murdered. In China, between three and six millions of infants are annually destroyed, while the total infanticide record of the whole world is appalling. In Africa, now, human beings are dying by millions of the sleeping sickness.

More destructive of life than war, is industry. In all civilised countries great masses of people are crowded into slums and labour-ghettos, where disease festers, vice corrodes, and famine is chronic, and where they die more swiftly and in greater numbers than do the soldiers in our modern wars. The very infant mortality of a slum parish in the East End of London is three times that of a middle-class parish in the West End. In the United States, in the last fourteen years, a total of coal-miners, greater than our entire standing army, has been killed and injured. The United States Bureau of Labour states that during the year 1908, there were between 30,000 and 35,000 deaths of workers by accidents, while 200,000 more were injured. In fact, the safest place for a working-man is in the army. And even if that army be at the front, fighting in Cuba or South Africa, the soldier in the ranks has a better chance for life than the working-man at home.

And yet, despite this terrible roll of death, despite the enormous killing of the past and the enormous killing of the present, there are to-day alive on the planet a billion and three quarters of human beings. Our immediate conclusion is that man is exceedingly fecund and very tough. Never before have there been so many people in the world. In the past centuries the world's population has been smaller; in the future centuries it is destined to be larger. And this brings us to that old bugbear that has been so frequently laughed away and that still persists in raising its grisly head--namely, the doctrine of Malthus. While man's increasing efficiency of food-production, combined with colonisation of whole virgin continents, has for generations given the apparent lie to Malthus' mathematical statement of the Law of Population, nevertheless the essential significance of his doctrine remains and cannot be challenged. Population does press against subsistence. And no matter how rapidly subsistence increases, population is certain to catch up with it.

When man was in the hunting stage of development, wide areas were necessary for the maintenance of scant populations. With the shepherd stages, the means of subsistence being increased, a larger population was supported on the same territory. The agricultural stage gave support to a still larger population; and, to-day, with the increased food-getting efficiency of a machine civilisation, an even larger population is made possible. Nor is this theoretical. The population is here, a billion and three quarters of men, women, and children, and this vast population is increasing on itself by leaps and bounds.

A heavy European drift to the New World has gone on and is going on; yet Europe, whose population a century ago was 170,000,000, has to-day 500,000,000. At this rate of increase, provided that subsistence is not overtaken, a century from now the population of Europe will be 1,500,000,000. And be it noted of the present rate of increase in the United States that only one-third is due to immigration, while two-thirds is due to excess of births over deaths. And at this present rate of increase, the population of the United States will be 500,000,000 in less than a century from now.

Man, the hungry one, the killer, has always suffered for lack of room. The world has been chronically overcrowded. Belgium with her 572 persons to the square mile is no more crowded than was Denmark when it supported only

500 palaeolithic people. According to Mr. Woodruff, cultivated land will produce 1600 times as much food as hunting land. From the time of the Norman Conquest, for centuries Europe could support no more than 25 to the square mile. To-day Europe supports 81 to the square mile. The explanation of this is that for the several centuries after the Norman Conquest her population was saturated. Then, with the development of trading and capitalism, of exploration and exploitation of new lands, and with the invention of labour-saving machinery and the discovery and application of scientific principles, was brought about a tremendous increase in Europe's food-getting efficiency. And immediately her population sprang up.

According to the census of Ireland, of 1659, that country had a population of 500,000. One hundred and fifty years later, her population was 8,000,000. For many centuries the population of Japan was stationary. There seemed no way of increasing her food-getting efficiency. Then, sixty years ago, came Commodore Perry, knocking down her doors and letting in the knowledge and machinery of the superior food- getting efficiency of the Western world. Immediately upon this rise in subsistence began the rise of population; and it is only the other day that Japan, finding her population once again pressing against subsistence, embarked, sword in hand, on a westward drift in search of more room. And, sword in hand, killing and being killed, she has carved out for herself Formosa and Korea, and driven the vanguard of her drift far into the rich interior of Manchuria.

For an immense period of time China's population has remained at 400,000,000--the saturation point. The only reason that the Yellow River periodically drowns millions of Chinese is that there is no other land for those millions to farm. And after every such catastrophe the wave of human life rolls up and now millions flood out upon that precarious territory. They are driven to it, because they are pressed remorselessly against subsistence. It is inevitable that China, sooner or later, like Japan, will learn and put into application our own superior food-getting efficiency. And when that time comes, it is likewise inevitable that her population will increase by unguessed millions until it again reaches the saturation point. And then, inoculated with

Western ideas, may she not, like Japan, take sword in hand and start forth colossally on a drift of her own for more room? This is another reputed bogie-- the Yellow Peril; yet the men of China are only men, like any other race of men, and all men, down all history, have drifted hungrily, here, there and everywhere over the planet, seeking for something to eat. What other men do, may not the Chinese do?

But a change has long been coming in the affairs of man. The more recent drifts of the stronger races, carving their way through the lesser breeds to more earth-space, has led to peace, ever to wider and more lasting peace. The lesser breeds, under penalty of being killed, have been compelled to lay down their weapons and cease killing among themselves. The scalp-talking Indian and the head-hunting Melanesian have been either destroyed or converted to a belief in the superior efficacy of civil suits and criminal prosecutions. The planet is being subdued. The wild and the hurtful are either tamed or eliminated. From the beasts of prey and the cannibal humans down to the death-dealing microbes, no quarter is given; and daily, wider and wider areas of hostile territory, whether of a warring desert-tribe in Africa or a pestilential fever-hole like Panama, are made peaceable and habitable for mankind. As for the great mass of stay-at-home folk, what percentage of the present generation in the United States, England, or Germany, has seen war or knows anything of war at first hand? There was never so much peace in the world as there is to-day.

War itself, the old red anarch, is passing. It is safer to be a soldier than a working-man. The chance for life is greater in an active campaign than in a factory or a coal-mine. In the matter of killing, war is growing impotent, and this in face of the fact that the machinery of war was never so expensive in the past nor so dreadful. War-equipment to- day, in time of peace, is more expensive than of old in time of war. A standing army costs more to maintain than it used to cost to conquer an empire. It is more expensive to be ready to kill, than it used to be to do the killing. The price of a Dreadnought would furnish the whole army of Xerxes with killing weapons. And, in spite of its magnificent equipment, war no longer kills as it used to when its methods were simpler. A bombardment by a modern fleet has been known to result in the killing of one mule. The casualties of a twentieth century war between two world-powers are such as to make a worker in an iron-foundry turn green with envy. War has become a joke. Men have made for themselves monsters of battle which they cannot face in battle. Subsistence is generous these days, life is not cheap, and it is not in the nature of flesh and blood to indulge in the carnage made possible by present-day machinery. This is not theoretical, as will be shown by a comparison of deaths in battle and men involved, in the South African War and the Spanish-American War on the one hand, and the Civil War or the Napoleonic Wars on the other.

Not only has war, by its own evolution, rendered itself futile, but man himself, with greater wisdom and higher ethics, is opposed to war. He has learned too much. War is repugnant to his common sense. He conceives it to be wrong, to be absurd, and to be very expensive. For the damage wrought and the results accomplished, it is not worth the price. Just as in the disputes of individuals the arbitration of a civil court instead of a blood feud is more practical, so, man decides, is arbitration more practical in the disputes of nations.

War is passing, disease is being conquered, and man's food-getting efficiency is increasing. It is because of these factors that there are a billion and three quarters of people alive to-day instead of a billion, or three-quarters of a billion. And it is because of these factors that the world's population will very soon be two billions and climbing rapidly toward three billions. The lifetime of the generation is increasing steadily. Men live longer these days. Life is not so precarious. The newborn infant has a greater chance for survival than at any time in the past. Surgery and sanitation reduce the fatalities that accompany the mischances of life and the ravages of disease. Men and women, with deficiencies and weaknesses that in the past would have effected their rapid extinction, live to-day and father and mother a numerous progeny. And high as the food-getting efficiency may soar, population is bound to soar after it. "The abysmal fecundity" of life has not altered. Given the food, and life will increase. A small percentage of the billion and three-quarters that live to-day may hush the clamour of life to be born, but it is only a small percentage. In this particular, the life in the man-animal is very like the life in the other animals.

And still another change is coming in human affairs. Though politicians gnash their teeth and cry anathema, and man, whose superficial book-learning is vitiated by crystallised prejudice, assures us that civilisation will go to smash, the trend of society, to-day, the world over, is toward socialism. The old individualism is passing. The state interferes more and more in affairs that hitherto have been considered sacredly private. And socialism, when the last word is said, is merely a new economic and political system whereby more men can get food to eat. In short, socialism is an improved food-getting efficiency.

Furthermore, not only will socialism get food more easily and in greater quantity, but it will achieve a more equitable distribution of that food. Socialism promises, for a time, to give all men, women, and children all they want to eat, and to enable them to eat all they want as often as they want. Subsistence will be pushed back, temporarily, an exceedingly long way. In consequence, the flood of life will rise like a tidal wave. There will be more marriages and more children born. The enforced sterility that obtains to-day for many millions, will no longer obtain. Nor will the fecund millions in the slums and labour-ghettos, who to-day die of all the ills due to chronic underfeeding and overcrowding, and who die with their fecundity largely unrealised, die in that future day when the increased food-getting efficiency of socialism will give them all they want to eat.

It is undeniable that population will increase prodigiously-just as it has increased prodigiously during the last few centuries, following upon the increase in food-getting efficiency. The magnitude of population in that future day is well nigh unthinkable. But there is only so much land and water on the surface of the earth. Man, despite his marvellous accomplishments, will never be able to increase the diameter of the planet. The old days of virgin continents will be gone. The habitable planet, from ice-cap to ice-cap, will be inhabited. And in the matter of food-getting, as in everything else, man is only finite. Undreamed-of efficiencies in food-getting may be achieved, but, soon or late, man will find himself face to face with Malthus' grim law. Not only will population catch up with subsistence, but it will press against subsistence, and the pressure will be pitiless and savage. Somewhere in the future is a date when man will face, consciously, the bitter fact that there is not food enough for all of him to eat.

When this day comes, what then? Will there be a recrudescence of old obsolete war? In a saturated population life is always cheap, as it is cheap in China, in India, to-day. Will new human drifts take place, questing for room, carving earth-space out of crowded life. Will the Sword again sing:

"Follow, O follow, then, Heroes, my harvesters! Where the tall grain is ripe Thrust in your sickles! Stripped and adust In a stubble of empire Scything and binding The full sheaves of sovereignty."

Even if, as of old, man should wander hungrily, sword in hand, slaying and being slain, the relief would be only temporary. Even if one race alone should hew down the last survivor of all the other races, that one race, drifting the world around, would saturate the planet with its own life and again press against subsistence. And in that day, the death rate and the birth rate will have to balance. Men will have to die, or be prevented from being born. Undoubtedly a higher quality of life will obtain, and also a slowly decreasing fecundity. But this decrease will be so slow that the pressure against subsistence will remain. The control of progeny will be one of the most important problems of man and one of the most important functions of the state. Men will simply be not permitted to be born.

Disease, from time to time, will ease the pressure. Diseases are parasites, and it must not be forgotten that just as there are drifts in the world of man, so are there drifts in the world of micro-organisms-- hunger-quests for food. Little is known of the micro-organic world, but that little is appalling; and no census of it will ever be taken, for there is the true, literal "abysmal fecundity." Multitudinous as man is, all his totality of individuals is as nothing in comparison with the inconceivable vastness of numbers of the micro-organisms. In your body, or in mine, right now, are swarming more individual entities than there are human beings in the world to-day. It is to us an invisible world. We only guess its nearest confines. With our powerful microscopes and ultramicroscopes, enlarging diameters twenty thousand times, we catch but the slightest glimpses of that profundity of infinitesimal life.

Little is known of that world, save in a general way. We know that out of it arise diseases, new to us, that afflict and destroy man. We do not know whether these diseases are merely the drifts, in a fresh direction, of already-existing breeds of micro-organisms, or whether they are new, absolutely new, breeds themselves just spontaneously generated. The latter hypothesis is tenable, for we theorise that if spontaneous generation still occurs on the earth, it is far more likely to occur in the form of simple organisms than of complicated organisms.

Another thing we know, and that is that it is in crowded populations that new diseases arise. They have done so in the past. They do so to-day. And no matter how wise are our physicians and bacteriologists, no matter how successfully they cope with these invaders, new invaders continue to arise-- new drifts of hungry life seeking to devour us. And so we are justified in believing that in the saturated populations of the future, when life is suffocating in the pressure against subsistence, that new, and ever new, hosts of destroying micro-organisms will continue to arise and fling themselves upon earth-crowded man to give him room. There may even be plagues of unprecedented ferocity that will depopulate great areas before the wit of man can overcome them. And this we know: that no matter how often these invisible hosts may be overcome by man's becoming immune to them through a cruel and terrible selection, new hosts will ever arise of these micro-organisms that were in the world before he came and that will be here after he is gone.

After he is gone? Will he then some day be gone, and this planet know him no more? Is it thither that the human drift in all its totality is trending? God Himself is silent on this point, though some of His prophets have given us vivid representations of that last day when the earth shall pass into nothingness. Nor does science, despite its radium speculations and its attempted analyses of the ultimate nature of matter, give us any other word than that man will pass. So far as man's knowledge goes, law is universal. Elements react under certain unchangeable conditions. One of these conditions is temperature. Whether it be in the test tube of the laboratory or the workshop of nature, all organic chemical reactions take place only within a restricted range of heat. Man, the latest of the ephemera, is pitifully a creature of temperature, strutting his brief day on the thermometer. Behind him is a past wherein it was too warm for him to exist. Ahead of him is a future wherein it will be too cold for him to exist. He cannot adjust himself to that future, because he cannot alter universal law, because he cannot alter his own construction nor the molecules that compose him.

It would be well to ponder these lines of Herbert Spencer's which follow, and which embody, possibly, the wildest vision the scientific mind has ever achieved:

"Motion as well as Matter being fixed in quantity, it would seem that the change in the distribution of Matter which Motion effects, coming to a limit in whichever direction it is carried, the indestructible Motion thereupon necessitates a reverse distribution. Apparently, the universally-co-existent forces of attraction and repulsion, which, as we have seen, necessitate rhythm in all minor changes throughout the Universe, also necessitate rhythm in the totality of its changes--produce now an immeasurable period during which the attractive forces predominating, cause universal concentration, and then an immeasurable period during which the repulsive forces predominating, cause universal diffusion--alternate eras of Evolution and Dissolution. _And thus there is suggested the conception of a past during which there have been successive Evolutions analogous to that which is now going on; a future during which successive other Evolutions may go on--ever the same in principle but never the same in concrete result_."

That is it--the most we know--alternate eras of evolution and dissolution. In the past there have been other evolutions similar to that one in which we live, and in the future there may be other similar evolutions--that is all. The principle of all these evolutions remains, but the concrete results are never twice alike. Man was not; he was; and again he will not be. In eternity which is beyond our comprehension, the particular evolution of that solar satellite we call the "Earth" occupied but a slight fraction of time. And of that fraction of time man occupies but a small portion. All the whole human drift, from the first ape-man to the last savant, is but a phantom, a flash of light and a flutter of movement across the infinite face of the starry night.

When the thermometer drops, man ceases--with all his lusts and wrestlings and achievements; with all his race-adventures and race-tragedies; and with all his red killings, billions upon billions of human lives multiplied by as many billions more. This is the last word of Science, unless there be some further, unguessed word which Science will some day find and utter. In the meantime it sees no farther than the starry void, where the "fleeting systems lapse like foam." Of what ledger-account is the tiny life of man in a vastness where stars snuff out like candles and great suns blaze for a time-tick of eternity and are gone?

And for us who live, no worse can happen than has happened to the earliest drifts of man, marked to-day by ruined cities of forgotten civilisation--ruined cities, which, on excavation, are found to rest on ruins of earlier cities, city upon city, and fourteen cities, down to a stratum where, still earlier, wandering herdsmen drove their flocks, and where, even preceding them, wild hunters chased their prey long after the cave-man and the man of the squatting-place cracked the knuckle-bones of wild animals and vanished from the earth. There is nothing terrible about it. With Richard Hovey, when he faced his death, we can say: "Behold! I have lived!" And with another and greater one, we can lay ourselves down with a will. The one drop of living, the one taste of being, has been good; and perhaps our greatest achievement will be that we dreamed immortality, even though we failed to realise it.

SMALL-BOAT SAILING

A sailor is born, not made. And by "sailor" is meant, not the average efficient and hopeless creature who is found to-day in the forecastle of deepwater ships, but the man who will take a fabric compounded of wood and iron and rope and canvas and compel it to obey his will on the surface of the sea. Barring captains and mates of big ships, the small- boat sailor is the real sailor. He knows--he must know--how to make the wind carry his craft from one given point to another given point. He must know about tides and rips and eddies, bar and channel markings, and day and night signals; he must be wise in weather-lore; and he must be sympathetically familiar with the peculiar qualities of his boat which differentiate it from every other boat that was ever built and rigged. He must know how to gentle her about, as one instance of a myriad, and to fill her on the other tack without deadening her way or allowing her to fall off too far.

The deepwater sailor of to-day needs know none of these things. And he doesn't. He pulls and hauls as he is ordered, swabs decks, washes paint, and chips iron-rust. He knows nothing, and cares less. Put him in a small boat and he is helpless. He will cut an even better figure on the hurricane deck of a horse.

I shall never forget my child-astonishment when I first encountered one of these strange beings. He was a runaway English sailor. I was a lad of twelve, with a decked-over, fourteen-foot, centre-board skiff which I had taught myself to sail. I sat at his feet as at the feet of a god, while he discoursed of strange lands and peoples, deeds of violence, and hair-raising gales at sea. Then, one day, I took him for a sail. With all the trepidation of the veriest little amateur, I hoisted sail and got under way. Here was a man, looking on critically, I was sure, who knew more in one second about boats and the water than I could ever know. After an interval, in which I exceeded myself, he took the tiller and the sheet. I sat on the little thwart amidships, open-mouthed, prepared to learn what real sailing was. My mouth remained open, for I learned what a real sailor was in a small boat. He couldn't trim the sheet to save himself, he nearly capsized several times in squalls, and, once again, by blunderingly jibing over; he didn't know what a centre-board was for, nor did he know that in running a boat before the wind one must sit in the middle instead of on the side; and finally, when we came back to the wharf, he ran the skiff in full tilt, shattering her nose and carrying away the mast-step. And yet he was a really truly sailor fresh from the vasty deep.

Which points my moral. A man can sail in the forecastles of big ships all his life and never know what real sailing is. From the time I was twelve, I listened to the lure of the sea. When I was fifteen I was captain and owner of an oyster-pirate sloop. By the time I was sixteen I was sailing in scow-schooners, fishing salmon with the Greeks up the Sacramento River, and serving as sailor on the Fish Patrol. And I was a good sailor, too, though all my cruising had been on San Francisco Bay and the rivers tributary to it. I had never been on the ocean in my life.

Then, the month I was seventeen, I signed before the mast as an able seaman on a three-top-mast schooner bound on a seven-months' cruise across the Pacific and back again. As my shipmates promptly informed me, I had had my nerve with me to sign on as able seaman. Yet behold, I was an able seaman. I had graduated from the right school. It took no more than minutes to learn the names and uses of the few new ropes. It was simple. I did not do things blindly. As a small-boat sailor I had learned to reason out and know the why of everything. It is true, I had to learn how to steer by compass, which took maybe half a minute; but when it came to steering "full-and-by" and "close-and-by," I could beat the average of my shipmates, because that was the very way I had always sailed. Inside fifteen minutes I could box the compass around and back again. And there was little else to learn during that seven-months' cruise, except fancy rope-sailorising, such as the more complicated lanyard knots and the making of various kinds of sennit and rope-mats. The point of all of which is that it is by means of small-boat sailing that the real sailor is best schooled.

And if a man is a born sailor, and has gone to the school of the sea, never in all his life can he get away from the sea again. The salt of it is in his bones as well as his nostrils, and the sea will call to him until he dies. Of late years, I have found easier ways of earning a living. I have quit the forecastle for keeps, but always I come back to the sea. In my case it is usually San Francisco Bay, than which no lustier, tougher, sheet of water can be found for small-boat sailing.

It really blows on San Francisco Bay. During the winter, which is the best cruising season, we have southeasters, southwesters, and occasional howling northers. Throughout the summer we have what we call the "sea-breeze," an unfailing wind off the Pacific that on most afternoons in the week blows what the Atlantic Coast yachtsmen would name a gale. They are always surprised by the small spread of canvas our yachts carry. Some of them, with schooners they have sailed around the Horn, have looked proudly at their own lofty sticks and huge spreads, then patronisingly and even pityingly at ours. Then, perchance, they have joined in a club cruise from San Francisco to Mare Island. They found the morning run up the Bay delightful. In the afternoon, when the brave west wind ramped across San Pablo Bay and they faced it on the long beat home, things were somewhat different. One by one, like a flight of swallows, our more meagrely sparred and canvassed yachts went by, leaving them wallowing and dead and shortening down in what they called a gale but which we called a dandy sailing breeze. The next time they came out, we would notice their sticks cut down, their booms shortened, and their after-leeches nearer the luffs by whole cloths.

As for excitement, there is all the difference in the world between a ship in trouble at sea, and a small boat in trouble on land-locked water. Yet for genuine excitement and thrill, give me the small boat. Things happen so quickly, and there are always so few to do the work--and hard work, too, as the small-boat sailor knows. I have toiled all night, both watches on deck, in a typhoon off the coast of Japan, and been less exhausted than by two hours' work at reefing down a thirty-foot sloop and heaving up two anchors on a lee shore in a screaming southeaster.

Hard work and excitement? Let the wind baffle and drop in a heavy tide- way just as you are sailing your little sloop through a narrow draw-bridge. Behold your sails, upon which you are depending, flap with sudden emptiness, and then see the impish wind, with a haul of eight points, fill your jib aback with a gusty puff. Around she goes, and sweeps, not through the open draw, but broadside on against the solid piles. Hear the roar of the tide, sucking through the trestle. And hear and see your pretty, fresh-painted boat crash against the piles. Feel her stout little hull give to the impact. See the rail actually pinch in. Hear your canvas tearing, and see the black, square-ended timbers thrusting holes through it. Smash! There goes your topmast stay, and the topmast reels over drunkenly above you. There is a ripping and crunching. If it continues, your starboard shrouds will be torn out. Grab a rope--any rope--and take a turn around a pile. But the free end of the rope is too short. You can't make it fast, and you hold on and wildly yell for your one companion to get a turn with another and longer rope. Hold on! You hold on till you are purple in the face, till it seems your arms are dragging out of their sockets, till the blood bursts from the ends of your fingers. But you hold, and your partner gets the longer rope and makes it fast. You straighten up and look at your hands. They are ruined. You can scarcely relax the crooks of the fingers. The pain is sickening. But there is no time. The skiff, which is always perverse, is pounding against the barnacles on the piles which threaten to scrape its gunwale off. It's drop the peak! Down jib! Then you run lines, and pull and haul and heave, and exchange unpleasant remarks with the bridge-tender who is always willing to meet you more than half way in such repartee. And finally, at the end of an hour, with aching back, sweat-soaked shirt, and slaughtered hands, you are through and swinging along on the placid, beneficent tide between narrow banks where the cattle stand knee-deep and gaze wonderingly at you. Excitement! Work! Can you beat it in a calm day on the deep sea?

I've tried it both ways. I remember labouring in a fourteen days' gale off the coast of New Zealand. We were a tramp collier, rusty and battered, with six thousand tons of coal in our hold. Life lines were stretched fore and aft; and on our weather side, attached to smokestack guys and rigging, were huge ropenettings, hung there for the purpose of breaking the force of the seas and so saving our mess-room doors. But the doors were smashed and the mess-rooms washed out just the same. And yet, out of it all, arose but the one feeling, namely, of monotony.

In contrast with the foregoing, about the liveliest eight days of my life were spent in a small boat on the west coast of Korea. Never mind why I was thus voyaging up the Yellow Sea during the month of February in below- zero weather. The point is that I was in an open boat, a sampan, on a rocky coast where there were no light-houses and where the tides ran from thirty to sixty feet. My crew were Japanese fishermen. We did not speak each other's language. Yet there was nothing monotonous about that trip. Never shall I forget one particular cold bitter dawn, when, in the thick of driving snow, we took in sail and dropped our small anchor. The wind was howling out of the northwest, and we were on a lee shore. Ahead and astern, all escape was cut off by rocky headlands, against whose bases burst the unbroken seas. To windward a short distance, seen only between the snow-squalls, was a low rocky reef. It was this that inadequately protected us from the whole Yellow Sea that thundered in upon us.

The Japanese crawled under a communal rice mat and went to sleep. I joined them, and for several hours we dozed fitfully. Then a sea deluged us out with icy water, and we found several inches of snow on top the mat. The reef to windward was disappearing under the rising tide, and moment by moment the seas broke more strongly over the rocks. The fishermen studied the shore anxiously. So did I, and with a sailor's eye, though I could see little chance for a swimmer to gain that surf- hammered line of rocks. I made signs toward the headlands on either flank. The Japanese shook their heads. I indicated that dreadful lee shore. Still they shook their heads and did nothing. My conclusion was that they were paralysed by the hopelessness of the situation. Yet our extremity increased with every minute, for the rising tide was robbing us of the reef that served as buffer. It soon became a case of swamping at our anchor. Seas were splashing on board in growing volume, and we baled constantly. And still my fishermen crew eyed the surf-battered shore and did nothing.

At last, after many narrow escapes from complete swamping, the fishermen got into action. All hands tailed on to the anchor and hove it up. For'ard, as the boat's head paid off, we set a patch of sail about the size of a flour-sack. And we headed straight for shore. I unlaced my shoes, unbottoned my great-coat and coat, and was ready to make a quick partial strip a minute or so before we struck. But we didn't strike, and, as we rushed in, I saw the beauty of the situation. Before us opened a narrow channel, frilled at its mouth with breaking seas. Yet, long before, when I had scanned the shore closely, there had been no such channel. I had forgotten the thirty-foot tide. And it was for this tide that the Japanese had so precariously waited. We ran the frill of breakers, curved into a tiny sheltered bay where the water was scarcely flawed by the gale, and landed on a beach where the salt sea of the last tide lay frozen in long curving lines. And this was one gale of three in the course of those eight days in the sampan. Would it have been beaten on a ship? I fear me the ship would have gone aground on the outlying reef and that its people would have been incontinently and monotonously drowned.

There are enough surprises and mishaps in a three-days' cruise in a small boat to supply a great ship on the ocean for a full year. I remember, once, taking out on her trial trip a little thirty-footer I had just bought. In six days we had two stiff blows, and, in addition, one proper southwester and one rip-snorting southeaster. The slight intervals between these blows were dead calms. Also, in the six days, we were aground three times. Then, too, we tied up to the bank in the Sacramento River, and, grounding by an accident on the steep slope on a falling tide, nearly turned a side somersault down the bank. In a stark calm and heavy tide in the Carquinez Straits, where anchors skate on the channel-scoured bottom, we were sucked against a big dock and smashed and bumped down a quarter of a mile of its length before we could get clear. Two hours afterward, on San Pablo Bay, the wind was piping up and we were reefing down. It is no fun to pick up a skiff adrift in a heavy sea and gale. That was our next task, for our skiff, swamping, parted both towing painters we had bent on. Before we recovered it we had nearly killed ourselves with exhaustion, and we certainly had strained the sloop in every part from keelson to truck. And to cap it all, coming into our home port, beating up the narrowest part of the San Antonio Estuary, we had a shave of inches from collision with a big ship in tow of a tug. I have sailed the ocean in far larger craft a year at a time, in which period occurred no such chapter of moving incident.

After all, the mishaps are almost the best part of small-boat sailing. Looking back, they prove to be punctuations of joy. At the time they try your mettle and your vocabulary, and may make you so pessimistic as to believe that God has a grudge against you--but afterward, ah, afterward, with what pleasure you remember them and with what gusto do you relate them to your brother skippers in the fellowhood of small-boat sailing!

A narrow, winding slough; a half tide, exposing mud surfaced with gangrenous slime; the water itself filthy and discoloured by the waste from the vats of a near-by tannery; the marsh grass on either side mottled with all the shades of a decaying orchid; a crazy, ramshackled, ancient wharf; and at the end of the wharf a small, white-painted sloop. Nothing romantic about it. No hint of adventure. A splendid pictorial argument against the alleged joys of small-boat sailing. Possibly that is what Cloudesley and I thought, that sombre, leaden morning as we turned out to cook breakfast and wash decks. The latter was my stunt, but one look at the dirty water overside and another at my fresh-painted deck, deterred me. After breakfast, we started a game of chess. The tide continued to fall, and we felt the sloop begin to list. We played on until the chess men began to fall over. The list increased, and we went on deck. Bow-line and stern-line were drawn taut. As we looked the boat listed still farther with an abrupt jerk. The lines were now very taut.

"As soon as her belly touches the bottom she will stop," I said.

Cloudesley sounded with a boat-hook along the outside.

"Seven feet of water," he announced. "The bank is almost up and down. The first thing that touches will be her mast when she turns bottom up."

An ominous, minute snapping noise came from the stern-line. Even as we looked, we saw a strand fray and part. Then we jumped. Scarcely had we bent another line between the stern and the wharf, when the original line parted. As we bent another line for'ard, the original one there crackled and parted. After that, it was an inferno of work and excitement.

We ran more and more lines, and more and more lines continued to part, and more and more the pretty boat went over on her side. We bent all our spare lines; we unrove sheets and halyards; we used our two-inch hawser; we fastened lines part way up the mast, half way up, and everywhere else. We toiled and sweated and enounced our mutual and sincere conviction that God's grudge still held against us. Country yokels came down on the wharf and sniggered at us. When Cloudesley let a coil of rope slip down the inclined deck into the vile slime and fished it out with seasick countenance, the yokels sniggered louder and it was all I could do to prevent him from climbing up on the wharf and committing murder.

By the time the sloop's deck was perpendicular, we had unbent the boom-lift from below, made it fast to the wharf, and, with the other end fast nearly to the mast-head, heaved it taut with block and tackle. The lift was of steel wire. We were confident that it could stand the strain, but we doubted the holding-power of the stays that held the mast.

The tide had two more hours to ebb (and it was the big run-out), which meant that five hours must elapse ere the returning tide would give us a chance to learn whether or not the sloop would rise to it and right herself.

The bank was almost up and down, and at the bottom, directly beneath us, the fast-ebbing tide left a pit of the vilest, illest-smelling, illest-appearing muck to be seen in many a day's ride. Said Cloudesley to me gazing down into it:

"I love you as a brother. I'd fight for you. I'd face roaring lions, and sudden death by field and flood. But just the same, don't you fall into that." He shuddered nauseously. "For if you do, I haven't the grit to pull you out. I simply couldn't. You'd be awful. The best I could do would be to take a boat-hook and shove you down out of sight."

We sat on the upper side-wall of the cabin, dangled our legs down the top of the cabin, leaned our backs against the deck, and played chess until the rising tide and the block and tackle on the boom-lift enabled us to get her on a respectable keel again. Years afterward, down in the South Seas, on the island of Ysabel, I was caught in a similar predicament. In order to clean her copper, I had careened the Snark broadside on to the beach and outward. When the tide rose, she refused to rise. The water crept in through the scuppers, mounted over the rail, and the level of the ocean slowly crawled up the slant of the deck. We battened down the engine-room hatch, and the sea rose to it and over it and climbed perilously near to the cabin companion-way and skylight. We were all sick with fever, but we turned out in the blazing tropic sun and toiled madly for several hours. We carried our heaviest lines ashore from our mast-heads and heaved with our heaviest purchase until everything crackled including ourselves. We would spell off and lie down like dead men, then get up and heave and crackle again. And in the end, our lower rail five feet under water and the wavelets lapping the companion-way combing, the sturdy little craft shivered and shook herself and pointed her masts once more to the zenith.

There is never lack of exercise in small-boat sailing, and the hard work is not only part of the fun of it, but it beats the doctors. San Francisco Bay is no mill pond. It is a large and draughty and variegated piece of water. I remember, one winter evening, trying to enter the mouth of the Sacramento. There was a freshet on the river, the flood tide from the bay had been beaten back into a strong ebb, and the lusty west wind died down with the sun. It was just sunset, and with a fair to middling breeze, dead aft, we stood still in the rapid current. We were squarely in the mouth of the river; but there was no anchorage and we drifted backward, faster and faster, and dropped anchor outside as the last breath of wind left us. The night came on, beautiful and warm and starry. My one companion cooked supper, while on deck I put everything in shape Bristol fashion. When we turned in at nine o'clock the weather- promise was excellent. (If I had carried a barometer I'd have known better.) By two in the morning our shrouds were thrumming in a piping breeze, and I got up and gave her more scope on her hawser. Inside another hour there was no doubt that we were in for a southeaster.

It is not nice to leave a warm bed and get out of a bad anchorage in a black blowy night, but we arose to the occasion, put in two reefs, and started to heave up. The winch was old, and the strain of the jumping head sea was too much for it. With the winch out of commission, it was impossible to heave up by hand. We knew, because we tried it and slaughtered our hands. Now a sailor hates to lose an anchor. It is a matter of pride. Of course, we could have buoyed ours and slipped it. Instead, however, I gave her still more hawser, veered her, and dropped the second anchor.

There was little sleep after that, for first one and then the other of us would be rolled out of our bunks. The increasing size of the seas told us we were dragging, and when we struck the scoured channel we could tell by the feel of it that our two anchors were fairly skating across. It was a deep channel, the farther edge of it rising steeply like the wall of a canyon, and when our anchors started up that wall they hit in and held.

Yet, when we fetched up, through the darkness we could hear the seas breaking on the solid shore astern, and so near was it that we shortened the skiff's painter.

Daylight showed us that between the stern of the skiff and destruction was no more than a score of feet. And how it did blow! There were times, in the gusts, when the wind must have approached a velocity of seventy or eighty miles an hour. But the anchors held, and so nobly that our final anxiety was that the for'ard bitts would be jerked clean out of the boat. All day the sloop alternately ducked her nose under and sat down on her stern; and it was not till late afternoon that the storm broke in one last and worst mad gust. For a full five minutes an absolute dead calm prevailed, and then, with the suddenness of a thunderclap, the wind snorted out of the southwest--a shift of eight points and a boisterous gale. Another night of it was too much for us, and we hove up by hand in a cross head-sea. It was not stiff work. It was heart-breaking. And I know we were both near to crying from the hurt and the exhaustion. And when we did get the first anchor up-and-down we couldn't break it out. Between seas we snubbed her nose down to it, took plenty of turns, and stood clear as she jumped. Almost everything smashed and parted except the anchor-hold. The chocks were jerked out, the rail torn off, and the very covering-board splintered, and still the anchor held. At last, hoisting the reefed mainsail and slacking off a few of the hard-won feet of the chain, we sailed the anchor out. It was nip and tuck, though, and there were times when the boat was knocked down flat. We repeated the manoeuvre with the remaining anchor, and in the gathering darkness fled into the shelter of the river's mouth.

I was born so long ago that I grew up before the era of gasolene. As a result, I am old-fashioned. I prefer a sail-boat to a motor-boat, and it is my belief that boat-sailing is a finer, more difficult, and sturdier art than running a motor. Gasolene engines are becoming fool-proof, and while it is unfair to say that any fool can run an engine, it is fair to say that almost any one can. Not so, when it comes to sailing a boat. More skill, more intelligence, and a vast deal more training are necessary. It is the finest training in the world for boy and youth and man. If the boy is very small, equip him with a small, comfortable skiff. He will do the rest. He won't need to be taught. Shortly he will be setting a tiny leg-of-mutton and steering with an oar. Then he will begin to talk keels and centreboards and want to take his blankets out and stop aboard all night.

But don't be afraid for him. He is bound to run risks and encounter accidents. Remember, there are accidents in the nursery as well as out on the water. More boys have died from hot-house culture than have died on boats large and small; and more boys have been made into strong and reliant men by boat-sailing than by lawn-croquet and dancing-school.

And once a sailor, always a sailor. The savour of the salt never stales. The sailor never grows so old that he does not care to go back for one more wrestling bout with wind and wave. I know it of myself. I have turned rancher, and live beyond sight of the sea. Yet I can stay away from it only so long.

After several months have passed, I begin to grow restless. I find myself daydreaming over incidents of the last cruise, or wondering if the striped bass are running on Wingo Slough, or eagerly reading the newspapers for reports of the first northern flights of ducks. And then, suddenly, there is a hurried pack of suit-cases and overhauling of gear, and we are off for Vallejo where the little Roamer lies, waiting, always waiting, for the skiff to come alongside, for the lighting of the fire in the galley-stove, for the pulling off of gaskets, the swinging up of the mainsail, and the rat-tat-tat of the reef-points, for the heaving short and the breaking out, and for the twirling of the wheel as she fills away and heads up Bay or down.

JACK LONDON On Board Roamer, Sonoma Creek, April 15, 1911

FOUR HORSES AND A SAILOR

"Huh! Drive four horses! I wouldn't sit behind you--not for a thousand dollars--over them mountain roads."

So said Henry, and he ought to have known, for he drives four horses himself.

Said another Glen Ellen friend: "What? London? He drive four horses? Can't drive one!"

And the best of it is that he was right. Even after managing to get a few hundred miles with my four horses, I don't know how to drive one. Just the other day, swinging down a steep mountain road and rounding an abrupt turn, I came full tilt on a horse and buggy being driven by a woman up the hill. We could not pass on the narrow road, where was only a foot to spare, and my horses did not know how to back, especially up- hill. About two hundred yards down the hill was a spot where we could pass. The driver of the buggy said she didn't dare back down because she was not sure of the brake. And as I didn't know how to tackle one horse, I didn't try it. So we unhitched her horse and backed down by hand. Which was very well, till it came to hitching the horse to the buggy again. She didn't know how. I didn't either, and I had depended on her knowledge. It took us about half an hour, with frequent debates and consultations, though it is an absolute certainty that never in its life was that horse hitched in that particular way.

No; I can't harness up one horse. But I can four, which compels me to back up again to get to my beginning. Having selected Sonoma Valley for our abiding place, Charmian and I decided it was about time we knew what we had in our own county and the neighbouring ones. How to do it, was the first question. Among our many weaknesses is the one of being old-fashioned. We don't mix with gasolene very well. And, as true sailors should, we naturally gravitate toward horses. Being one of those lucky individuals who carries his office under his hat, I should have to take a typewriter and a load of books along. This put saddle-horses out of the running. Charmian suggested driving a span. She had faith in me; besides, she could drive a span herself. But when I thought of the many mountains to cross, and of crossing them for three months with a poor tired span, I vetoed the proposition and said we'd have to come back to gasolene after all. This she vetoed just as emphatically, and a deadlock obtained until I received inspiration.

"Why not drive four horses?" I said.

"But you don't know how to drive four horses," was her objection.

I threw my chest out and my shoulders back. "What man has done, I can do," I proclaimed grandly. "And please don't forget that when we sailed on the Snark I knew nothing of navigation, and that I taught myself as I sailed."

"Very well," she said. (And there's faith for you!) "They shall be four saddle horses, and we'll strap our saddles on behind the rig."

It was my turn to object. "Our saddle horses are not broken to harness."

"Then break them."

And what I knew about horses, much less about breaking them, was just about as much as any sailor knows. Having been kicked, bucked off, fallen over backward upon, and thrown out and run over, on very numerous occasions, I had a mighty vigorous respect for horses; but a wife's faith must be lived up to, and I went at it.

King was a polo pony from St. Louis, and Prince a many-gaited love-horse from Pasadena. The hardest thing was to get them to dig in and pull. They rollicked along on the levels and galloped down the hills, but when they struck an up-grade and felt the weight of the breaking-cart, they stopped and turned around and looked at me. But I passed them, and my troubles began. Milda was fourteen years old, an unadulterated broncho, and in temperament was a combination of mule and jack-rabbit blended equally. If you pressed your hand on her flank and told her to get over, she lay down on you. If you got her by the head and told her to back, she walked forward over you. And if you got behind her and shoved and told her to "Giddap!" she sat down on you. Also, she wouldn't walk. For endless weary miles I strove with her, but never could I get her to walk a step. Finally, she was a manger-glutton. No matter how near or far from the stable, when six o'clock came around she bolted for home and never missed the directest cross-road. Many times I rejected her.

The fourth and most rejected horse of all was the Outlaw. From the age of three to seven she had defied all horse-breakers and broken a number of them. Then a long, lanky cowboy, with a fifty-pound saddle and a Mexican bit had got her proud goat. I was the next owner. She was my favourite riding horse. Charmian said I'd have to put her in as a wheeler where I would have more control over her. Now Charmian had a favourite riding mare called Maid. I suggested Maid as a substitute. Charmian pointed out that my mare was a branded range horse, while hers was a near-thoroughbred, and that the legs of her mare would be ruined forever if she were driven for three months. I acknowledged her mare's thoroughbredness, and at the same time defied her to find any thoroughbred with as small and delicately-viciously pointed ears as my Outlaw. She indicated Maid's exquisitely thin shinbone. I measured the Outlaw's. It was equally thin, although, I insinuated, possibly more durable. This stabbed Charmian's pride. Of course her near-thoroughbred Maid, carrying the blood of "old" Lexington, Morella, and a streak of the super-enduring Morgan, could run, walk, and work my unregistered Outlaw into the ground; and that was the very precise reason why such a paragon of a saddle animal should not be degraded by harness.

So it was that Charmian remained obdurate, until, one day, I got her behind the Outlaw for a forty-mile drive. For every inch of those forty miles the Outlaw kicked and jumped, in between the kicks and jumps finding time and space in which to seize its team-mate by the back of the neck and attempt to drag it to the ground. Another trick the Outlaw developed during that drive was suddenly to turn at right angles in the traces and endeavour to butt its team-mate over the grade. Reluctantly and nobly did Charmian give in and consent to the use of Maid. The Outlaw's shoes were pulled off, and she was turned out on range.

Finally, the four horses were hooked to the rig--a light Studebaker trap. With two hours and a half of practice, in which the excitement was not abated by several jack-poles and numerous kicking matches, I announced myself as ready for the start. Came the morning, and Prince, who was to have been a wheeler with Maid, showed up with a badly kicked shoulder. He did not exactly show up; we had to find him, for he was unable to walk. His leg swelled and continually swelled during the several days we waited for him. Remained only the Outlaw. In from pasture she came, shoes were nailed on, and she was harnessed into the wheel. Friends and relatives strove to press accident policies on me, but Charmian climbed up alongside, and Nakata got into the rear seat with the typewriter--Nakata, who sailed cabin-boy on the Snark for two years and who had shown himself afraid of nothing, not even of me and my amateur jamborees in experimenting with new modes of locomotion. And we did very nicely, thank you, especially after the first hour or so, during which time the Outlaw had kicked about fifty various times, chiefly to the damage of her own legs and the paintwork, and after she had bitten a couple of hundred times, to the damage of Maid's neck and Charmian's temper. It was hard enough to have her favourite mare in the harness without also enduring the spectacle of its being eaten alive.

Our leaders were joys. King being a polo pony and Milda a rabbit, they rounded curves beautifully and darted ahead like coyotes out of the way of the wheelers. Milda's besetting weakness was a frantic desire not to have the lead-bar strike her hocks. When this happened, one of three things occurred: either she sat down on the lead-bar, kicked it up in the air until she got her back under it, or exploded in a straight-ahead, harness-disrupting jump. Not until she carried the lead-bar clean away and danced a break-down on it and the traces, did she behave decently. Nakata and I made the repairs with good old-fashioned bale-rope, which is stronger than wrought-iron any time, and we went on our way.

In the meantime I was learning--I shall not say to tool a four-in-hand--but just simply to drive four horses. Now it is all right enough to begin with four work-horses pulling a load of several tons. But to begin with four light horses, all running, and a light rig that seems to outrun them--well, when things happen they happen quickly. My weakness was total ignorance. In particular, my fingers lacked training, and I made the mistake of depending on my eyes to handle the reins. This brought me up against a disastrous optical illusion. The bight of the off head-line, being longer and heavier than that of the off wheel-line, hung lower. In a moment requiring quick action, I invariably mistook the two lines. Pulling on what I thought was the wheel-line, in order to straighten the team, I would see the leaders swing abruptly around into a jack-pole. Now for sensations of sheer impotence, nothing can compare with a jack-pole, when the horrified driver beholds his leaders prancing gaily up the road and his wheelers jogging steadily down the road, all at the same time and all harnessed together and to the same rig.

I no longer jack-pole, and I don't mind admitting how I got out of the habit. It was my eyes that enslaved my fingers into ill practices. So I shut my eyes and let the fingers go it alone. To-day my fingers are independent of my eyes and work automatically. I do not see what my fingers do. They just do it. All I see is the satisfactory result.

Still we managed to get over the ground that first day--down sunny Sonoma Valley to the old town of Sonoma, founded by General Vallejo as the remotest outpost on the northern frontier for the purpose of holding back the Gentiles, as the wild Indians of those days were called. Here history was made. Here the last Spanish mission was reared; here the Bear flag was raised; and here Kit Carson, and Fremont, and all our early adventurers came and rested in the days before the days of gold.

We swung on over the low, rolling hills, through miles of dairy farms and chicken ranches where every blessed hen is white, and down the slopes to Petaluma Valley. Here, in 1776, Captain Quiros came up Petaluma Creek from San Pablo Bay in quest of an outlet to Bodega Bay on the coast. And here, later, the Russians, with Alaskan hunters, carried skin boats across from Fort Ross to poach for sea-otters on the Spanish preserve of San Francisco Bay. Here, too, still later, General Vallejo built a fort, which still stands--one of the finest examples of Spanish adobe that remain to us. And here, at the old fort, to bring the chronicle up to date, our horses proceeded to make peculiarly personal history with astonishing success and dispatch. King, our peerless, polo-pony leader, went lame. So hopelessly lame did he go that no expert, then and afterward, could determine whether the lameness was in his frogs, hoofs, legs, shoulders, or head. Maid picked up a nail and began to limp. Milda, figuring the day already sufficiently spent and maniacal with manger-gluttony, began to rabbit-jump. All that held her was the bale- rope. And the Outlaw, game to the last, exceeded all previous exhibitions of skin-removing, paint-marring, and horse-eating.

At Petaluma we rested over while King was returned to the ranch and Prince sent to us. Now Prince had proved himself an excellent wheeler, yet he had to go into the lead and let the Outlaw retain his old place. There is an axiom that a good wheeler is a poor leader. I object to the last adjective. A good wheeler makes an infinitely worse kind of a leader than that. I know . . . now. I ought to know. Since that day I have driven Prince a few hundred miles in the lead. He is neither any better nor any worse than the first mile he ran in the lead; and his worst is even extremely worse than what you are thinking. Not that he is vicious. He is merely a good-natured rogue who shakes hands for sugar, steps on your toes out of sheer excessive friendliness, and just goes on loving you in your harshest moments.

But he won't get out of the way. Also, whenever he is reproved for being in the wrong, he accuses Milda of it and bites the back of her neck. So bad has this become that whenever I yell "Prince!" in a loud voice, Milda immediately rabbit-jumps to the side, straight ahead, or sits down on the lead-bar. All of which is quite disconcerting. Picture it yourself. You are swinging round a sharp, down-grade, mountain curve, at a fast trot. The rock wall is the outside of the curve. The inside of the curve is a precipice. The continuance of the curve is a narrow, unrailed bridge. You hit the curve, throwing the leaders in against the wall and making the polo-horse do the work. All is lovely. The leaders are hugging the wall like nestling doves. But the moment comes in the evolution when the leaders must shoot out ahead. They really must shoot, or else they'll hit the wall and miss the bridge. Also, behind them are the wheelers, and the rig, and you have just eased the brake in order to put sufficient snap into the manoeuvre. If ever team-work is required, now is the time. Milda tries to shoot. She does her best, but Prince, bubbling over with roguishness, lags behind. He knows the trick. Milda is half a length ahead of him. He times it to the fraction of a second. Maid, in the wheel, over-running him, naturally bites him. This disturbs the Outlaw, who has been behaving beautifully, and she immediately reaches across for Maid. Simultaneously, with a fine display of firm conviction that it's all Milda's fault, Prince sinks his teeth into the back of Milda's defenceless neck. The whole thing has occurred in less than a second. Under the surprise and pain of the bite, Milda either jumps ahead to the imminent peril of harness and lead-bar, or smashes into the wall, stops short with the lead-bar over her back, and emits a couple of hysterical kicks. The Outlaw invariably selects this moment to remove paint. And after things are untangled and you have had time to appreciate the close shave, you go up to Prince and reprove him with your choicest vocabulary. And Prince, gazelle-eyed and tender, offers to shake hands with you for sugar. I leave it to any one: a boat would never act that way.

We have some history north of the Bay. Nearly three centuries and a half ago, that doughty pirate and explorer, Sir Francis Drake, combing the Pacific for Spanish galleons, anchored in the bight formed by Point Reyes, on which to-day is one of the richest dairy regions in the world. Here, less than two decades after Drake, Sebastien Carmenon piled up on the rocks with a silk-laden galleon from the Philippines. And in this same bay of Drake, long afterward, the Russian fur-poachers rendezvous'd their bidarkas and stole in through the Golden Gate to the forbidden waters of San Francisco Bay.

Farther up the coast, in Sonoma County, we pilgrimaged to the sites of the Russian settlements. At Bodega Bay, south of what to-day is called Russian River, was their anchorage, while north of the river they built their fort. And much of Fort Ross still stands. Log-bastions, church, and stables hold their own, and so well, with rusty hinges creaking, that we warmed ourselves at the hundred-years-old double fireplace and slept under the hand-hewn roof beams still held together by spikes of hand-wrought iron.

We went to see where history had been made, and we saw scenery as well. One of our stretches in a day's drive was from beautiful Inverness on Tomales Bay, down the Olema Valley to Bolinas Bay, along the eastern shore of that body of water to Willow Camp, and up over the sea-bluffs, around the bastions of Tamalpais, and down to Sausalito. From the head of Bolinas Bay to Willow Camp the drive on the edge of the beach, and actually, for half-mile stretches, in the waters of the bay itself, was a delightful experience. The wonderful part was to come. Very few San Franciscans, much less Californians, know of that drive from Willow Camp, to the south and east, along the poppy-blown cliffs, with the sea thundering in the sheer depths hundreds of feet below and the Golden Gate opening up ahead, disclosing smoky San Francisco on her many hills. Far off, blurred on the breast of the sea, can be seen the Farallones, which Sir Francis Drake passed on a S. W. course in the thick of what he describes as a "stynking fog." Well might he call it that, and a few other names, for it was the fog that robbed him of the glory of discovering San Francisco Bay.

It was on this part of the drive that I decided at last I was learning real mountain-driving. To confess the truth, for delicious titillation of one's nerve, I have since driven over no mountain road that was worse, or better, rather, than that piece.

And then the contrast! From Sausalito, over excellent, park-like boulevards, through the splendid redwoods and homes of Mill Valley, across the blossomed hills of Marin County, along the knoll-studded picturesque marshes, past San Rafael resting warmly among her hills, over the divide and up the Petaluma Valley, and on to the grassy feet of Sonoma Mountain and home. We covered fifty-five miles that day. Not so bad, eh, for Prince the Rogue, the paint-removing Outlaw, the thin-shanked thoroughbred, and the rabbit-jumper? And they came in cool and dry, ready for their mangers and the straw.

Oh, we didn't stop. We considered we were just starting, and that was many weeks ago. We have kept on going over six counties which are comfortably large, even for California, and we are still going. We have twisted and tabled, criss-crossed our tracks, made fascinating and lengthy dives into the interior valleys in the hearts of Napa and Lake Counties, travelled the coast for hundreds of miles on end, and are now in Eureka, on Humboldt Bay, which was discovered by accident by the gold-seekers, who were trying to find their way to and from the Trinity diggings. Even here, the white man's history preceded them, for dim tradition says that the Russians once anchored here and hunted sea-otter before the first Yankee trader rounded the Horn, or the first Rocky Mountain trapper thirsted across the "Great American Desert" and trickled down the snowy Sierras to the sun-kissed land. No; we are not resting our horses here on Humboldt Bay. We are writing this article, gorging on abalones and mussels, digging clams, and catching record-breaking sea-trout and rock-cod in the intervals in which we are not sailing, motor-boating, and swimming in the most temperately equable climate we have ever experienced.

These comfortably large counties! They are veritable empires. Take Humboldt, for instance. It is three times as large as Rhode Island, one and a half times as large as Delaware, almost as large as Connecticut, and half as large as Massachusetts. The pioneer has done his work in this north of the bay region, the foundations are laid, and all is ready for the inevitable inrush of population and adequate development of resources which so far have been no more than skimmed, and casually and carelessly skimmed at that. This region of the six counties alone will some day support a population of millions. In the meanwhile, O you home- seekers, you wealth-seekers, and, above all, you climate-seekers, now is the time to get in on the ground floor.

Robert Ingersoll once said that the genial climate of California would in a fairly brief time evolve a race resembling the Mexicans, and that in two or three generations the Californians would be seen of a Sunday morning on their way to a cockfight with a rooster under each arm. Never was made a rasher generalisation, based on so absolute an ignorance of facts. It is to laugh. Here is a climate that breeds vigour, with just sufficient geniality to prevent the expenditure of most of that vigour in fighting the elements. Here is a climate where a man can work three hundred and sixty-five days in the year without the slightest hint of enervation, and where for three hundred and sixty-five nights he must perforce sleep under blankets. What more can one say? I consider myself somewhat of climate expert, having adventured among most of the climates of five out of the six zones. I have not yet been in the Antarctic, but whatever climate obtains there will not deter me from drawing the conclusion that nowhere is there a climate to compare with that of this region. Maybe I am as wrong as Ingersoll was. Nevertheless I take my medicine by continuing to live in this climate. Also, it is the only medicine I ever take.

But to return to the horses. There is some improvement. Milda has actually learned to walk. Maid has proved her thoroughbredness by never tiring on the longest days, and, while being the strongest and highest spirited of all, by never causing any trouble save for an occasional kick at the Outlaw. And the Outlaw rarely gallops, no longer butts, only periodically kicks, comes in to the pole and does her work without attempting to vivisect Maid's medulla oblongata, and--marvel of marvels--is really and truly getting lazy. But Prince remains the same incorrigible, loving and lovable rogue he has always been.

And the country we've been over! The drives through Napa and Lake Counties! One, from Sonoma Valley, via Santa Rosa, we could not refrain from taking several ways, and on all the ways we found the roads excellent for machines as well as horses. One route, and a more delightful one for an automobile cannot be found, is out from Santa Rosa, past old Altruria and Mark West Springs, then to the right and across to Calistoga in Napa Valley. By keeping to the left, the drive holds on up the Russian River Valley, through the miles of the noted Asti Vineyards to Cloverdale, and then by way of Pieta, Witter, and Highland Springs to Lakeport. Still another way we took, was down Sonoma Valley, skirting San Pablo Bay, and up the lovely Napa Valley. From Napa were side excursions through Pope and Berryessa Valleys, on to AEtna Springs, and still on, into Lake County, crossing the famous Langtry Ranch.

Continuing up the Napa Valley, walled on either hand by great rock palisades and redwood forests and carpeted with endless vineyards, and crossing the many stone bridges for which the County is noted and which are a joy to the beauty-loving eyes as well as to the four-horse tyro driver, past Calistoga with its old mud-baths and chicken-soup springs, with St. Helena and its giant saddle ever towering before us, we climbed the mountains on a good grade and dropped down past the quicksilver mines to the canyon of the Geysers. After a stop over night and an exploration of the miniature-grand volcanic scene, we pulled on across the canyon and took the grade where the cicadas simmered audibly in the noon sunshine among the hillside manzanitas. Then, higher, came the big cattle-dotted upland pastures, and the rocky summit. And here on the summit, abruptly, we caught a vision, or what seemed a mirage. The ocean we had left long days before, yet far down and away shimmered a blue sea, framed on the farther shore by rugged mountains, on the near shore by fat and rolling farm lands. Clear Lake was before us, and like proper sailors we returned to our sea, going for a sail, a fish, and a swim ere the day was done and turning into tired Lakeport blankets in the early evening. Well has Lake

County been called the Walled-in County. But the railroad is coming. They say the approach we made to Clear Lake is similar to the approach to Lake Lucerne. Be that as it may, the scenery, with its distant snow-capped peaks, can well be called Alpine.

And what can be more exquisite than the drive out from Clear Lake to Ukiah by way of the Blue Lakes chain!--every turn bringing into view a picture of breathless beauty; every glance backward revealing some perfect composition in line and colour, the intense blue of the water margined with splendid oaks, green fields, and swaths of orange poppies. But those side glances and backward glances were provocative of trouble. Charmian and I disagreed as to which way the connecting stream of water ran. We still disagree, for at the hotel, where we submitted the affair to arbitration, the hotel manager and the clerk likewise disagreed. I assume, now, that we never will know which way that stream runs. Charmian suggests "both ways." I refuse such a compromise. No stream of water I ever saw could accomplish that feat at one and the same time. The greatest concession I can make is that sometimes it may run one way and sometimes the other, and that in the meantime we should both consult an oculist.

More valley from Ukiah to Willits, and then we turned westward through the virgin Sherwood Forest of magnificent redwood, stopping at Alpine for the night and continuing on through Mendocino County to Fort Bragg and "salt water." We also came to Fort Bragg up the coast from Fort Ross, keeping our coast journey intact from the Golden Gate. The coast weather was cool and delightful, the coast driving superb. Especially in the Fort Ross section did we find the roads thrilling, while all the way along we followed the sea. At every stream, the road skirted dizzy cliff- edges, dived down into lush growths of forest and ferns and climbed out along the cliff-edges again. The way was lined with flowers--wild lilac, wild roses, poppies, and lupins. Such lupins!--giant clumps of them, of every lupin-shade and--colour. And it was along the Mendocino roads that Charmian caused many delays by insisting on getting out to pick the wild blackberries, strawberries, and thimble-berries which grew so profusely. And ever we caught peeps, far down, of steam schooners loading lumber in the rocky coves; ever we skirted the cliffs, day after day, crossing stretches of rolling farm lands and passing through thriving villages and sawmill towns. Memorable was our launch-trip from Mendocino City up Big River, where the steering gears of the launches work the reverse of anywhere else in the world; where we saw a stream of logs, of six to twelve and fifteen feet in diameter, which filled the river bed for miles to the obliteration of any sign of water; and where we were told of a white or albino redwood tree. We did not see this last, so cannot vouch for it.

All the streams were filled with trout, and more than once we saw the side-hill salmon on the slopes. No, side-hill salmon is not a peripatetic fish; it is a deer out of season. But the trout! At Gualala Charmian caught her first one. Once before in my life I had caught two . . . on angleworms. On occasion I had tried fly and spinner and never got a strike, and I had come to believe that all this talk of fly-fishing was just so much nature-faking. But on the Gualala River I caught trout--a lot of them--on fly and spinners; and I was beginning to feel quite an expert, until Nakata, fishing on bottom with a pellet of bread for bait, caught the biggest trout of all. I now affirm there is nothing in science nor in art. Nevertheless, since that day poles and baskets have been added to our baggage, we tackle every stream we come to, and we no longer are able to remember the grand total of our catch.

At Usal, many hilly and picturesque miles north of Fort Bragg, we turned again into the interior of Mendocino, crossing the ranges and coming out in Humboldt County on the south fork of Eel River at Garberville. Throughout the trip, from Marin County north, we had been warned of "bad roads ahead." Yet we never found those bad roads. We seemed always to be just ahead of them or behind them. The farther we came the better the roads seemed, though this was probably due to the fact that we were learning more and more what four horses and a light rig could do on a road. And thus do I save my face with all the counties. I refuse to make invidious road comparisons. I can add that while, save in rare instances on steep pitches, I have trotted my horses down all the grades, I have never had one horse fall down nor have I had to send the rig to a blacksmith shop for repairs.

Also, I am learning to throw leather. If any tyro thinks it is easy to take a short-handled, long-lashed whip, and throw the end of that lash just where he wants it, let him put on automobile goggles and try it. On reconsideration, I would suggest the substitution of a wire fencing-mask for the goggles. For days I looked at that whip. It fascinated me, and the fascination was composed mostly of fear. At my first attempt, Charmian and Nakata became afflicted with the same sort of fascination, and for a long time afterward, whenever they saw me reach for the whip, they closed their eyes and shielded their heads with their arms.

Here's the problem. Instead of pulling honestly, Prince is lagging back and manoeuvring for a bite at Milda's neck. I have four reins in my hands. I must put these four reins into my left hand, properly gather the whip handle and the bight of the lash in my right hand, and throw that lash past Maid without striking her and into Prince. If the lash strikes Maid, her thoroughbredness will go up in the air, and I'll have a case of horse hysteria on my hands for the next half hour. But follow. The whole problem is not yet stated. Suppose that I miss Maid and reach the intended target. The instant the lash cracks, the four horses jump, Prince most of all, and his jump, with spread wicked teeth, is for the back of Milda's neck. She jumps to escape--which is her second jump, for the first one came when the lash exploded. The Outlaw reaches for Maid's neck, and Maid, who has already jumped and tried to bolt, tries to bolt harder. And all this infinitesimal fraction of time I am trying to hold the four animals with my left hand, while my whip-lash, writhing through the air, is coming back to me. Three simultaneous things I must do: keep hold of the four reins with my left hand; slam on the brake with my foot; and on the rebound catch that flying lash in the hollow of my right arm and get the bight of it safely into my right hand. Then I must get two of the four lines back into my right hand and keep the horses from running away or going over the grade. Try it some time. You will find life anything but wearisome. Why, the first time I hit the mark and made the lash go off like a revolver shot, I was so astounded and delighted that I was paralysed. I forgot to do any of the multitudinous other things, tangled the whip lash in Maid's harness, and was forced to call upon Charmian for assistance. And now, confession. I carry a few pebbles handy. They're great for reaching Prince in a tight place. But just the same I'm learning that whip every day, and before I get home I hope to discard the pebbles. And as long as I rely on pebbles, I cannot truthfully speak of myself as "tooling a four-in-hand."

From Garberville, where we ate eel to repletion and got acquainted with the aborigines, we drove down the Eel River Valley for two days through the most unthinkably glorious body of redwood timber to be seen anywhere in California. From Dyerville on to Eureka, we caught glimpses of railroad construction and of great concrete bridges in the course of building, which advertised that at least Humboldt County was going to be linked to the rest of the world.

We still consider our trip is just begun. As soon as this is mailed from Eureka, it's heigh ho! for the horses and pull on. We shall continue up the coast, turn in for Hoopa Reservation and the gold mines, and shoot down the Trinity and Klamath rivers in Indian canoes to Requa. After that, we shall go on through Del Norte County and into Oregon. The trip so far has justified us in taking the attitude that we won't go home until the winter rains drive us in. And, finally, I am going to try the experiment of putting the Outlaw in the lead and relegating Prince to his old position in the near wheel. I won't need any pebbles then.

NOTHING THAT EVER CAME TO ANYTHING

It was at Quito, the mountain capital of Ecuador, that the following passage at correspondence took place. Having occasion to buy a pair of shoes in a shop six feet by eight in size and with walls three feet thick, I noticed a mangy leopard skin on the floor. I had no Spanish. The shop-keeper had no English. But I was an adept at sign language. I wanted to know where I should go to buy leopard skins. On my scribble-pad I drew the interesting streets of a city. Then I drew a small shop, which, after much effort, I persuaded the proprietor into recognising as his shop. Next, I indicated in my drawing that on the many streets there were many shops. And, finally, I made myself into a living interrogation mark, pointing all the while from the mangy leopard skin to the many shops I had sketched.

But the proprietor failed to follow me. So did his assistant. The street came in to help--that is, as many as could crowd into the six-by- eight shop; while those that could not force their way in held an overflow meeting on the sidewalk. The proprietor and the rest took turns at talking to me in rapid-fire Spanish, and, from the expressions on their faces, all concluded that I was remarkably stupid. Again I went through my programme, pointing on the sketch from the one shop to the many shops, pointing out that in this particular shop was one leopard skin, and then questing interrogatively with my pencil among all the shops. All regarded me in blank silence, until I saw comprehension suddenly dawn on the face of a small boy.

"Tigres montanya!" he cried.

This appealed to me as mountain tigers, namely, leopards; and in token that he understood, the boy made signs for me to follow him, which I obeyed. He led me for a quarter of a mile, and paused before the doorway of a large building where soldiers slouched on sentry duty and in and out of which went other soldiers. Motioning for me to remain, he ran inside.

Fifteen minutes later he was out again, without leopard skins, but full of information. By means of my card, of my hotel card, of my watch, and of the boy's fingers, I learned the following: that at six o'clock that evening he would arrive at my hotel with ten leopard skins for my inspection. Further, I learned that the skins were the property of one Captain Ernesto Becucci. Also, I learned that the boy's name was Eliceo.

The boy was prompt. At six o'clock he was at my room. In his hand was a small roll addressed to me. On opening it I found it to be manuscript piano music, the Hora Tranquila Valse, or "Tranquil Hour Waltz," by Ernesto

Becucci. I came for leopard skins, thought I, and the owner sends me sheet music instead. But the boy assured me that he would have the skins at the hotel at nine next morning, and I entrusted to him the following letter of acknowledgment:

"DEAR CAPTAIN BECUCCI:

"A thousand thanks for your kind presentation of _Hora Tranquila Valse_. Mrs. London will play it for me this evening.

"Sincerely yours,

"Jack London."

Next morning Eliceo was back, but without the skins. Instead, he gave me a letter, written in Spanish, of which the following is a free translation:

"To my dearest and always appreciated friend, I submit myself--

"DEAR SIR:

"I sent you last night an offering by the bearer of this note, and you returned me a letter which I translated.

"Be it known to you, sir, that I am giving this waltz away in the best society, and therefore to your honoured self. Therefore it is beholden to you to recognise the attention, I mean by a tangible return, as this composition was made by myself. You will therefore send by your humble servant, the bearer, any offering, however minute, that you may be prompted to make. Send it under cover of an envelope. The bearer may be trusted.

"I did not indulge in the pleasure of visiting your honourable self this morning, as I find my body not to be enjoying the normal exercise of its functions.

"As regards the skins from the mountain, you shall be waited on by a small boy at seven o'clock at night with ten skins from which you may select those which most satisfy your aspirations.

"In the hope that you will look upon this in the same light as myself, I beg to be allowed to remain,

"Your most faithful servant,

"CAPTAIN ERNESTO BECUCCI."

Well, thought I, this Captain Ernesto Becucci has shown himself to be such an undependable person, that, while I don't mind rewarding him for his composition, I fear me if I do I never shall lay eyes on those leopard skins. So to Eliceo I gave this letter for the Captain:

"MY DEAR CAPTAIN BECUCCI:

"Have the boy bring the skins at seven o'clock this evening, when I shall be glad to look at them. This evening when the boy brings the skins, I shall be pleased to give him, in an envelope, for you, a tangible return for your musical composition.

"Please put the price on each skin, and also let me know for what sum all the skins will sell together.

"Sincerely yours,

"JACK LONDON."

Now, thought I, I have him. No skins, no tangible return; and evidently he is set on receiving that tangible return.

At seven o'clock Eliceo was back, but without leopard skins. He handed me this letter:

"SENOR LONDON:

"I wish to instil in you the belief that I lost to-day, at half past three in the afternoon, the key to my cubicle. While distributing rations to the soldiers I dropped it. I see in this loss the act of God.

"I received a letter from your honourable self, delivered by the one who bears you this poor response of mine. To-morrow I will burst open the door to permit me to keep my word with you. I feel myself eternally shamed not to be able to dominate the evils that afflict colonial mankind. Please send me the trifle that you offered me. Send me this proof of your appreciation by the bearer, who is to be trusted. Also give to him a small sum of money for himself, and earn the undying gratitude of

"Your most faithful servant,

"CAPTAIN ERNESTO BECUCCI."

Also, inclosed in the foregoing letter was the following original poem, a propos neither of leopard skins nor tangible returns, so far as I can make out:

EFFUSION

Thou canst not weep; Nor ask I for a year To rid me of my woes Or make my life more dear.

The mystic chains that bound Thy all-fond heart to mine, Alas! asundered are For now and for all time.

In vain you strove to hide, From vulgar gaze of man, The burning glance of love That none but Love can scan.

Go on thy starlit way And leave me to my fate; Our souls must needs unite-- But, God! 'twill be too late.

To all and sundry of which I replied:

"MY DEAR CAPTAIN BECUCCI:

"I regret exceedingly to hear that by act of God, at half past three this afternoon, you lost the key to your cubicle. Please have the boy bring the skins at seven o'clock to-morrow morning, at which time, when he brings the skins, I shall be glad to make you that tangible return for your 'Tranquil Hour Waltz.'

"Sincerely yours,

"JACK LONDON."

At seven o'clock came no skins, but the following:

"SIR:

"After offering you my most sincere respects, I beg to continue by telling you that no one, up to the time of writing, has treated me with such lack of attention. It was a present to gentlemen who were to retain the piece of music, and who have all, without exception, made me a present of five dollars. It is beyond my humble capacity to believe that you, after having offered to send me money in an envelope, should fail to do so.

"Send me, I pray of you, the money to remunerate the small boy for his repeated visits to you. Please be discreet and send it in an envelope by the bearer.

"Last night I came to the hotel with the boy. You were dining. I waited more than an hour for you and then went to the theatre. Give the boy some small amount, and send me a like offering of larger proportions.

"Awaiting incessantly a slight attention on your part,

"CAPTAIN ERNESTO BECUCCI."

And here, like one of George Moore's realistic studies, ends this intercourse with Captain Ernesto Becucci. Nothing happened. Nothing ever came to anything. He got no tangible return, and I got no leopard skins. The tangible return he might have got, I presented to Eliceo, who promptly invested it in a pair of trousers and a ticket to the bull-fight.

(NOTE TO EDITOR.--This is a faithful narration of what actually happened in Quito, Ecuador.)

THAT DEAD MEN RISE UP NEVER

The month in which my seventeenth birthday arrived I signed on before the mast on the Sophie Sutherland, a three-topmast schooner bound on a seven-months' seal-hunting cruise to the coast of Japan. We sailed from San Francisco, and immediately I found confronting me a problem of no inconsiderable proportions. There were twelve men of us in the forecastle, ten of whom were hardened, tarry-thumbed sailors. Not alone was I a youth and on my first voyage, but I had for shipmates men who had come through the hard school of the merchant service of Europe. As boys, they had had to perform their ship's duty, and, in addition, by immemorial sea custom, they had had to be the slaves of the ordinary and able-bodied seamen. When they became ordinary seamen they were still the slaves of the able-bodied. Thus, in the forecastle, with the watch below, an able seaman, lying in his bunk, will order an ordinary seaman to fetch him his shoes or bring him a drink of water. Now the ordinary seaman may be lying in his bunk. He is just as tired as the able seaman. Yet he must get out of his bunk and fetch and carry. If he refuses, he will be beaten. If, perchance, he is so strong that he can whip the able seaman, then all the able seamen, or as many as may be necessary, pitch upon the luckless devil and administer the beating.

My problem now becomes apparent. These hard-bit Scandinavian sailors had come through a hard school. As boys they had served their mates, and as able seamen they looked to be served by other boys. I was a boy--withal with a man's body. I had never been to sea before--withal I was a good sailor and knew my business. It was either a case of holding my own with them or of going under. I had signed on as an equal, and an equal I must maintain myself, or else endure seven months of hell at their hands. And it was this very equality they resented. By what right was I an equal? I had not earned that high privilege. I had not endured the miseries they had endured as maltreated boys or bullied ordinaries. Worse than that, I was a land-lubber making his first voyage. And yet, by the injustice of fate, on the ship's articles I was their equal.

My method was deliberate, and simple, and drastic. In the first place, I resolved to do my work, no matter how hard or dangerous it might be, so well that no man would be called upon to do it for me. Further, I put ginger in my muscles. I never malingered when pulling on a rope, for I knew the eagle eyes of my forecastle mates were squinting for just such evidences of my inferiority. I made it a point to be among the first of the watch going on deck, among the last going below, never leaving a sheet or tackle for some one else to coil over a pin. I was always eager for the run aloft for the shifting of topsail sheets and tacks, or for the setting or taking in of topsails; and in these matters I did more than my share.

Furthermore, I was on a hair-trigger of resentment myself. I knew better than to accept any abuse or the slightest patronizing. At the first hint of such, I went off--I exploded. I might be beaten in the subsequent fight, but I left the impression that I was a wild-cat and that I would just as willingly fight again. My intention was to demonstrate that I would tolerate no imposition. I proved that the man who imposed on me must have a fight on his hands. And doing my work well, the innate justice of the men, assisted by their wholesome dislike for a clawing and rending wild-cat ruction, soon led them to give over their hectoring. After a bit of strife, my attitude was accepted, and it was my pride that I was taken in as an equal in spirit as well as in fact. From then on, everything was beautiful, and the voyage promised to be a happy one.

But there was one other man in the forecastle. Counting the Scandinavians as ten, and myself as the eleventh, this man was the twelfth and last. We never knew his name, contenting ourselves with calling him the "Bricklayer." He was from Missouri--at least he so informed us in the one meagre confidence he was guilty of in the early days of the voyage. Also, at that time, we learned several other things. He was a bricklayer by trade. He had never even seen salt water until the week before he joined us, at which time he had arrived in San Francisco and looked upon San Francisco Bay. Why he, of all men, at forty years of age, should have felt the prod to go to sea, was beyond all of us; for it was our unanimous conviction that no man less fitted for the sea had ever embarked on it. But to sea he had come. After a week's stay in a sailors' boarding-house, he had been shoved aboard of us as an able seaman.

All hands had to do his work for him. Not only did he know nothing, but he proved himself unable to learn anything. Try as they would, they could never teach him to steer. To him the compass must have been a profound and awful whirligig. He never mastered its cardinal points, much less the checking and steadying of the ship on her course. He never did come to know whether ropes should be coiled from left to right or from right to left. It was mentally impossible for him to learn the easy muscular trick of throwing his weight on a rope in pulling and hauling. The simplest knots and turns were beyond his comprehension, while he was mortally afraid of going aloft. Bullied by captain and mate, he was one day forced aloft. He managed to get underneath the crosstrees, and there he froze to the ratlines. Two sailors had to go after him to help him down.

All of which was bad enough had there been no worse. But he was vicious, malignant, dirty, and without common decency. He was a tall, powerful man, and he fought with everybody. And there was no fairness in his fighting. His first fight on board, the first day out, was with me, when he, desiring to cut a plug of chewing tobacco, took my personal table-knife for the purpose, and whereupon, I, on a hair-trigger, promptly exploded. After that he fought with nearly every member of the crew. When his clothing became too filthy to be bearable by the rest of us, we put it to soak and stood over him while he washed it. In short, the Bricklayer was one of those horrible and monstrous things that one must see in order to be convinced that they exist.

I will only say that he was a beast, and that we treated him like a beast. It is only by looking back through the years that I realise how heartless we were to him. He was without sin. He could not, by the very nature of things, have been anything else than he was. He had not made himself, and for his making he was not responsible. Yet we treated him as a free agent and held him personally responsible for all that he was and that he should not have been. As a result, our treatment of him was as terrible as he was himself terrible. Finally we gave him the silent treatment, and for weeks before he died we neither spoke to him nor did he speak to us. And for weeks he moved among us, or lay in his bunk in our crowded house, grinning at us his hatred and malignancy. He was a dying man, and he knew it, and we knew it. And furthermore, he knew that we wanted him to die. He cumbered our life with his presence, and ours was a rough life that made rough men of us. And so he died, in a small space crowded by twelve men and as much alone as if he had died on some desolate mountain peak. No kindly word, no last word, was passed between. He died as he had lived, a beast, and he died hating us and hated by us.

And now I come to the most startling moment of my life. No sooner was he dead than he was flung overboard. He died in a night of wind, drawing his last breath as the men tumbled into their oilskins to the cry of "All hands!" And he was flung overboard, several hours later, on a day of wind. Not even a canvas wrapping graced his mortal remains; nor was he deemed worthy of bars of iron at his feet. We sewed him up in the blankets in which he died and laid him on a hatch-cover for'ard of the main-hatch on the port side. A gunnysack, half full of galley coal, was fastened to his feet.

navigator of the present would be aghast if asked to voyage for two years, from Boston, around the Horn to California, and back again, without a chronometer. In those days such a proceeding was a matter of course, for those were the days when dead reckoning was indeed something to reckon on, when running down the latitude was a common way of finding a place, and when lunar observations were direly necessary. It may be fairly asserted that very few merchant officers of to-day ever make a lunar observation, and that a large percentage are unable to do it.

"Sept. 22nd., upon coming on deck at seven bells in the morning we found the other watch aloft throwing water upon the sails, and looking astern we saw a small, clipper-built brig with a black hull heading directly after us. We went to work immediately, and put all the canvas upon the brig which we could get upon her, rigging out oars for studding-sail yards; and contined wetting down the sails by buckets of water whipped up to the mast-head . . . She was armed, and full of men, and showed no colours."

The foregoing sounds like a paragraph from "Midshipman Easy" or the "Water Witch," rather than a paragraph from the soberest, faithfullest, and most literal chronicle of the sea ever written. And yet the chase by a pirate occurred, on board the brig Pilgrim, on September 22nd, 1834--something like only two generations ago.

Dana was the thorough-going type of man, not overbalanced and erratic, without quirk or quibble of temperament. He was efficient, but not brilliant. His was a general all-round efficiency. He was efficient at the law; he was efficient at college; he was efficient as a sailor; he was efficient in the matter of pride, when that pride was no more than the pride of a forecastle hand, at twelve dollars a month, in his seaman's task well done, in the smart sailing of his captain, in the clearness and trimness of his ship.

There is no sailor whose cockles of the heart will not warm to Dana's description of the first time he sent down a royal yard. Once or twice he had seen it done. He got an old hand in the crew to coach him. And then, the first anchorage at Monterey, being pretty thick with the second mate, he got him to ask the mate to be sent up the first time the royal yards were struck. "Fortunately," as Dana describes it, "I got through without any word from the officer; and heard the 'well done' of the mate, when the yard reached the deck, with as much satisfaction as I ever felt at Cambridge on seeing a 'bene' at the foot of a Latin exercise."

"This was the first time I had taken a weather ear-ring, and I felt not a little proud to sit astride of the weather yard-arm, past the ear-ring, and sing out 'Haul out to leeward!'" He had been over a year at sea before he essayed this able seaman's task, but he did it, and he did it with pride. And with pride, he went down a four-hundred foot cliff, on a pair of top-gallant studding-sail halyards bent together, to dislodge several dollars worth of stranded bullock hides, though all the acclaim he got from his mates was: "What a d-d fool you were to risk your life for half a dozen hides!"

In brief, it was just this efficiency in pride, as well as work, that enabled Dana to set down, not merely the photograph detail of life before the mast and hide-droghing on the coast of California, but of the untarnished simple psychology and ethics of the forecastle hands who droghed the hides, stood at the wheel, made and took in sail, tarred down the rigging, holystoned the decks, turned in all-standing, grumbled as they cut about the kid, criticised the seamanship of their officers, and estimated the duration of their exile from the cubic space of the hide- house.

JACK LONDON Glen Ellen, California, August 13, 1911.

A WICKED WOMAN (Curtain Raiser) BY JACK LONDON

Scene--California.

Time--Afternoon of a summer day.

CHARACTERS

LORETTA, A sweet, young thing. Frightfully innocent. About nineteen years old. Slender, delicate, a fragile flower. Ingenuous.

NED BASHFORD, A jaded young man of the world, who has philosophised his experiences and who is without faith in the veracity or purity of women.

BILLY MARSH, A boy from a country town who is just about as innocent as Loretta. Awkward. Positive. Raw and callow youth.

ALICE HEMINGWAY, A society woman, good-hearted, and a match-maker.

JACK HEMINGWAY, Her husband.

MAID.

A WICKED WOMAN

[Curtain rises on a conventional living room of a country house in California. It is the Hemingway house at Santa Clara. The room is remarkable for magnificent stone fireplace at rear centre. On either side of fireplace are generous, diamond-paned windows. Wide, curtained doorways to right and left. To left, front, table, with vase of flowers and chairs. To right, front, grand piano.]

[Curtain discovers LORETTA seated at piano, not playing, her back to it, facing NED BASHFORD, who is standing.]

LORETTA. [Petulantly, fanning herself with sheet of music.] No, I won't go fishing. It's too warm. Besides, the fish won't bite so early in the afternoon.

NED. Oh, come on. It's not warm at all. And anyway, we won't really fish. I want to tell you something.

LORETTA. [Still petulantly.] You are always wanting to tell me something.

NED. Yes, but only in fun. This is different. This is serious. Our . . . my happiness depends upon it.

LORETTA. [Speaking eagerly, no longer petulant, looking, serious and delighted, divining a proposal.] Then don't wait. Tell me right here.

NED. [Almost threateningly.] Shall I?

LORETTA. [Challenging.] Yes.

[He looks around apprehensively as though fearing interruption, clears his throat, takes resolution, also takes LORETTA's hand.]

[LORETTA is startled, timid, yet willing to hear, naively unable to conceal her love for him.]

NED. [Speaking softly.] Loretta . . . I, . . . ever since I met you I have--

[JACK HEMINGWAY appears in the doorway to the left, just entering.]

[NED suddenly drops LORETTA's hand. He shows exasperation.]

[LORETTA shows disappointment at interruption.]

NED. Confound it

LORETTA. [Shocked.] Ned! Why will you swear so?

NED. [Testily.] That isn't swearing.

LORETTA. What is it, pray?

NED. Displeasuring.

JACK HEMINGWAY. [Who is crossing over to right.] Squabbling again?

LORETTA. [Indignantly and with dignity.] No, we're not.

NED. [Gruffly.] What do you want now?

JACK HEMINGWAY. [Enthusiastically.] Come on fishing.

NED. [Snappily.] No. It's too warm.

JACK HEMINGWAY. [Resignedly, going out right.] You needn't take a fellow's head off.

LORETTA. I thought you wanted to go fishing.

NED. Not with Jack.

LORETTA. [Accusingly, fanning herself vigorously.] And you told me it wasn't warm at all.

NED. [Speaking softly.] That isn't what I wanted to tell you, Loretta. [He takes her hand.] Dear Loretta--

[Enter abruptly ALICE HEMINGWAY from right.]

[LORETTA sharply jerks her hand away, and looks put out.]

[NED tries not to look awkward.]

ALICE HEMINGWAY. Goodness! I thought you'd both gone fishing!

LORETTA. [Sweetly.] Is there anything you want, Alice?

NED. [Trying to be courteous.] Anything I can do?

ALICE HEMINGWAY. [Speaking quickly, and trying to withdraw.] No, no. I only came to see if the mail had arrived.

LORETTA AND NED

[Speaking together.] No, it hasn't arrived.

LORETTA. [Suddenly moving toward door to right.] I am going to see.

[NED looks at her reproachfully.]

[LORETTA looks back tantalisingly from doorway and disappears.]

[NED flings himself disgustedly into Morris chair.]

ALICE HEMINGWAY. [Moving over and standing in front of him. Speaks accusingly.] What have you been saying to her?

NED. [Disgruntled.] Nothing.

ALICE HEMINGWAY. [Threateningly.] Now listen to me, Ned.

NED. [Earnestly.] On my word, Alice, I've been saying nothing to her.

ALICE HEMINGWAY. [With sudden change of front.] Then you ought to have been saying something to her.

NED. [Irritably. Getting chair for her, seating her, and seating himself again.] Look here, Alice, I know your game. You invited me down here to make a fool of me.

ALICE HEMINGWAY. Nothing of the sort, sir. I asked you down to meet a sweet and unsullied girl--the sweetest, most innocent and ingenuous girl in the world.

NED. [Dryly.] That's what you said in your letter.

ALICE HEMINGWAY. And that's why you came. Jack had been trying for a year to get you to come. He did not know what kind of a letter to write.

NED. If you think I came because of a line in a letter about a girl I'd never seen--

ALICE HEMINGWAY. [Mockingly.] The poor, jaded, world-worn man, who is no longer interested in women . . . and girls! The poor, tired pessimist who has lost all faith in the goodness of women--

NED. For which you are responsible.

ALICE HEMINGWAY. [Incredulously.] I?

NED. You are responsible. Why did you throw me over and marry Jack?

ALICE HEMINGWAY. Do you want to know?

NED. Yes.

ALICE HEMINGWAY. [Judiciously.] First, because I did not love you. Second, because you did not love me. [She smiles at his protesting hand and at the protesting expression on his face.] And third, because there were just about twenty-seven other women at that time that you loved, or thought you loved. That is why I married Jack. And that is why you lost faith in the goodness of women. You have only yourself to blame.

NED. [Admiringly.] You talk so convincingly. I almost believe you as I listen to you. And yet I know all the time that you are like all the rest of your sex--faithless, unveracious, and . . .

[He glares at her, but does not proceed.]

ALICE HEMINGWAY. Go on. I'm not afraid.

NED. [With finality.] And immoral.

ALICE HEMINGWAY. Oh! You wretch!

NED. [Gloatingly.] That's right. Get angry. You may break the furniture if you wish. I don't mind.

ALICE HEMINGWAY. [With sudden change of front, softly.] And how about Loretta?

[NED gasps and remains silent.]

ALICE HEMINGWAY. The depths of duplicity that must lurk under that sweet and innocent exterior . . . according to your philosophy!

NED. [Earnestly.] Loretta is an exception, I confess. She is all that you said in your letter. She is a little fairy, an angel. I never dreamed of anything like her. It is remarkable to find such a woman in this age.

ALICE HEMINGWAY. [Encouragingly.] She is so naive.

NED. [Taking the bait.] Yes, isn't she? Her face and her tongue betray all her secrets.

ALICE HEMINGWAY. [Nodding her head.] Yes, I have noticed it.

NED. [Delightedly.] Have you?

ALICE HEMINGWAY. She cannot conceal anything. Do you know that she loves you?

NED. [Falling into the trap, eagerly.] Do you think so?

ALICE HEMINGWAY. [Laughing and rising.] And to think I once permitted you to make love to me for three weeks!

[NED rises.]

[MAID enters from left with letters, which she brings to ALICE HEMINGWAY.]

ALICE HEMINGWAY. [Running over letters.] None for you, Ned. [Selecting two letters for herself.] Tradesmen. [Handing remainder of letters to MAID.] And three for Loretta. [Speaking to MAID.] Put them on the table, Josie.

[MAID puts letters on table to left front, and makes exit to left.]

NED. [With shade of jealousy.] Loretta seems to have quite a correspondence.

ALICE HEMINGWAY. [With a sigh.] Yes, as I used to when I was a girl.

NED. But hers are family letters.

ALICE HEMINGWAY. Yes, I did not notice any from Billy.

NED. [Faintly.] Billy?

ALICE HEMINGWAY. [Nodding.] Of course she has told you about him?

NED. [Gasping.] She has had lovers . . . already?

ALICE HEMINGWAY. And why not? She is nineteen.

NED. [Haltingly.] This . . . er . . . this Billy . . . ?

ALICE HEMINGWAY. [Laughing and putting her hand reassuringly on his arm.] Now don't be alarmed, poor, tired philosopher. She doesn't love Billy at all.

[LORETTA enters from right.]

ALICE HEMINGWAY. [To LORETTA, nodding toward table.] Three letters for you.

LORETTA. [Delightedly.] Oh! Thank you.

[LORETTA trips swiftly across to table, looks at letters, sits down, opens letters, and begins to read.]

NED. [Suspiciously.] But Billy?

ALICE HEMINGWAY. I am afraid he loves her very hard. That is why she is here. They had to send her away. Billy was making life miserable for her. They were little children together--playmates. And Billy has been, well, importunate. And Loretta, poor child, does not know anything about marriage. That is all.

NED. [Reassured.] Oh, I see.

[ALICE HEMINGWAY starts slowly toward right exit, continuing conversation and accompanied by NED.]

ALICE HEMINGWAY. [Calling to LORETTA.] Are you going fishing, Loretta?

[LORETTA looks up from letter and shakes head.]

ALICE HEMINGWAY. [To NED.] Then you're not, I suppose?

NED. No, it's too warm.

ALICE HEMINGWAY. Then I know the place for you.

NED. Where?

ALICE HEMINGWAY. Right here. [Looks significantly in direction of LORETTA.] Now is your opportunity to say what you ought to say.

[ALICE HEMINGWAY laughs teasingly and goes out to right.]

[NED hesitates, starts to follow her, looks at LORETTA, and stops. He twists his moustache and continues to look at her meditatively.]

[LORETTA is unaware of his presence and goes on reading. Finishes letter, folds it, replaces in envelope, looks up, and discovers NED.]

LORETTA. [Startled.] Oh! I thought you were gone.

NED. [Walking across to her.] I thought I'd stay and finish our conversation.

LORETTA. [Willingly, settling herself to listen.] Yes, you were going to . . . [Drops eyes and ceases talking.]

NED. [Taking her hand, tenderly.] I little dreamed when I came down here visiting that I was to meet my destiny in--[Abruptly releases LORETTA's hand.]

[MAID enters from left with tray.]

[LORETTA glances into tray and discovers that it is empty. She looks inquiringly at MAID.]

MAID. A gentleman to see you. He hasn't any card. He said for me to tell you that it was Billy.

LORETTA. [Starting, looking with dismay and appeal to NED.] Oh! . . . Ned!

NED [Gracefully and courteously, rising to his feet and preparing to go.] If you'll excuse me now, I'll wait till afterward to tell you what I wanted.

LORETTA. [In dismay.] What shall I do?

NED. [Pausing.] Don't you want to see him? [LORETTA shakes her head.] Then don't.

LORETTA. [Slowly.] I can't do that. We are old friends. We . . . were children together. [To the MAID.] Send him in. [To NED, who has started to go out toward right.] Don't go, Ned.

[MAID makes exit to left.]

NED. [Hesitating a moment.] I'll come back.

[NED makes exit to right.]

[LORETTA, left alone on stage, shows perturbation and dismay.]

[BILLY enters from left. Stands in doorway a moment. His shoes are dusty. He looks overheated. His eyes and face brighten at sight of LORETTA.]

BILLY. [Stepping forward, ardently.] Loretta!

LORETTA. [Not exactly enthusiastic in her reception, going slowly to meet him.] You never said you were coming.

[BILLY shows that he expects to kiss her, but she merely shakes his hand.]

BILLY. [Looking down at his very dusty shoes.] I walked from the station.

LORETTA. If you had let me know, the carriage would have been sent for you.

BILLY. [With expression of shrewdness.] If I had let you know, you wouldn't have let me come.

[BILLY looks around stage cautiously, then tries to kiss her.]

LORETTA. [Refusing to be kissed.] Won't you sit down?

BILLY. [Coaxingly.] Go on, just one. [LORETTA shakes head and holds him off.] Why not? We're engaged.

LORETTA. [With decision.] We're not. You know we're not. You know I broke it off the day before I came away. And . . . and . . . you'd better sit down.

[BILLY sits down on edge of chair. LORETTA seats herself by table. Billy, without rising, jerks his chair forward till they are facing each other, his knees touching hers. He yearns toward her. She moves back her chair slightly.]

BILLY. [With supreme confidence.] That's what I came to see you for--to get engaged over again.

[BILLY hudges chair forward and tries to take her hand.]

[LORETTA hudges her chair back.]

BILLY. [Drawing out large silver watch and looking at it.] Now look here, Loretta, I haven't any time to lose. I've got to leave for that train in ten minutes. And I want you to set the day.

LORETTA. But we're not engaged, Billy. So there can't be any setting of the day.

BILLY. [With confidence.] But we're going to be. [Suddenly breaking out.] Oh, Loretta, if you only knew how I've suffered. That first night I didn't sleep a wink. I haven't slept much ever since. [Hudges chair forward.] I walk the floor all night. [Solemnly.] Loretta, I don't eat enough to keep a canary bird alive. Loretta . . . [Hudges chair forward.]

LORETTA. [Hudging her chair back maternally.] Billy, what you need is a tonic. Have you seen Doctor Haskins?

BILLY. [Looking at watch and evincing signs of haste.] Loretta, when a girl kisses a man, it means she is going to marry him.

LORETTA. I know it, Billy. But . . . [She glances toward letters on table.] Captain Kitt doesn't want me to marry you. He says . . . [She takes letter and begins to open it.]

BILLY. Never mind what Captain Kitt says. He wants you to stay and be company for your sister. He doesn't want you to marry me because he knows she wants to keep you.

LORETTA. Daisy doesn't want to keep me. She wants nothing but my own happiness. She says--[She takes second letter from table and begins to open it.]

BILLY. Never mind what Daisy says--

LORETTA. [Taking third letter from table and beginning to open it.] And Martha says--

BILLY. [Angrily.] Darn Martha and the whole boiling of them!

LORETTA. [Reprovingly.] Oh, Billy!

BILLY. [Defensively.] Darn isn't swearing, and you know it isn't.

[There is an awkward pause. Billy has lost the thread of the conversation and has vacant expression.]

BILLY. [Suddenly recollecting.] Never mind Captain Kitt, and Daisy, and Martha, and what they want. The question is, what do you want?

LORETTA. [Appealingly.] Oh, Billy, I'm so unhappy.

BILLY. [Ignoring the appeal and pressing home the point.] The thing is, do you want to marry me? [He looks at his watch.] Just answer that.

LORETTA. Aren't you afraid you'll miss that train?

BILLY. Darn the train!

LORETTA. [Reprovingly.] Oh, Billy!

BILLY. [Most irascibly.] Darn isn't swearing. [Plaintively.] That's the way you always put me off. I didn't come all the way here for a train. I came for you. Now just answer me one thing. Do you want to marry me?

LORETTA. [Firmly.] No, I don't want to marry you.

BILLY. [With assurance.] But you've got to, just the same.

LORETTA. [With defiance.] Got to?

BILLY. [With unshaken assurance.] That's what I said--got to. And I'll see that you do.

LORETTA. [Blazing with anger.] I am no longer a child. You can't bully me, Billy Marsh!

BILLY. [Coolly.] I'm not trying to bully you. I'm trying to save your reputation.

LORETTA. [Faintly.] Reputation?

BILLY. [Nodding.] Yes, reputation. [He pauses for a moment, then speaks very solemnly.] Loretta, when a woman kisses a man, she's got to marry him.

LORETTA. [Appalled, faintly.] Got to?

BILLY. [Dogmatically.] It is the custom.

LORETTA. [Brokenly.] And when . . . a . . . a woman kisses a man and doesn't . . . marry him . . . ?

BILLY. Then there is a scandal. That's where all the scandals you see in the papers come from.

[BILLY looks at watch.]

[LORETTA in silent despair.]

LORETTA. [In abasement.] You are a good man, Billy. [Billy shows that he believes it.] And I am a very wicked woman.

BILLY. No, you're not, Loretta. You just didn't know.

LORETTA. [With a gleam of hope.] But you kissed me first.

BILLY. It doesn't matter. You let me kiss you.

LORETTA. [Hope dying down.] But not at first.

BILLY. But you did afterward and that's what counts. You let me you in the grape-arbour. You let me--

LORETTA. [With anguish] Don't! Don't!

BILLY. [Relentlessly.]--kiss you when you were playing the piano. You let me kiss you that day of the picnic. And I can't remember all the times you let me kiss you good night.

LORETTA. [Beginning to weep.] Not more than five.

BILLY. [With conviction.] Eight at least.

LORETTA. [Reproachfully, still weeping.] You told me it was all right.

BILLY. [Emphatically.] So it was all right--until you said you wouldn't marry me after all. Then it was a scandal--only no one knows it yet. If you marry me no one ever will know it. [Looks at watch.] I've got to go. [Stands up.] Where's my hat?

LORETTA. [Sobbing.] This is awful.

BILLY. [Approvingly.] You bet it's awful. And there's only one way out. [Looks anxiously about for hat.] What do you say?

LORETTA. [Brokenly.] I must think. I'll write to you. [Faintly.] The train? Your hat's in the hall.

BILLY. [Looks at watch, hastily tries to kiss her, succeeds only in shaking hand, starts across stage toward left.] All right. You write to me. Write tomorrow. [Stops for a moment in doorway and speaks very solemnly.] Remember, Loretta, there must be no scandal.

[Billy goes out.]

[LORETTA sits in chair quietly weeping. Slowly dries eyes, rises from chair, and stands, undecided as to what she will do next.]

[NED enters from right, peeping. Discovers that LORETTA is alone, and comes quietly across stage to her. When NED comes up to her she begins weeping again and tries to turn her head away. NED catches both her hands in his and compels her to look at him. She weeps harder.]

NED. [Putting one arm protectingly around her shoulder and drawing her toward him.] There, there, little one, don't cry.

LORETTA. [Turning her face to his shoulder like a tired child, sobbing.] Oh, Ned, if you only knew how wicked I am.

NED. [Smiling indulgently.] What is the matter, little one? Has your dearly beloved sister failed to write to you? [LORETTA shakes head.] Has Hemingway been bullying you? [LORETTA shakes head.] Then it must have been that caller of yours? [Long pause, during which LORETTA's weeping grows more violent.] Tell me what's the matter, and we'll see what I can do. [He lightly kisses her hair--so lightly that she does not know.]

LORETTA. [Sobbing.] I can't. You will despise me. Oh, Ned, I am so ashamed.

NED. [Laughing incredulously.] Let us forget all about it. I want to tell you something that may make me very happy. My fondest hope is that it will make you happy, too. Loretta, I love you--

LORETTA. [Uttering a sharp cry of delight, then moaning.] Too late!

NED. [Surprised.] Too late?

LORETTA. [Still moaning.] Oh, why did I? [NED somewhat stiffens.] I was so young. I did not know the world then.

NED. What is it all about anyway?

LORETTA. Oh, I . . . he . . . Billy . . . I am a wicked woman, Ned. I know you will never speak to me again.

NED. This . . . er . . . this Billy--what has he been doing?

LORETTA. I . . . he . . . I didn't know. I was so young. I could not help it. Oh, I shall go mad, I shall go mad!

[NED's encircling arm goes limp. He gently disengages her and deposits her in big chair.]

[LORETTA buries her face and sobs afresh.]

NED. [Twisting moustache fiercely, regarding her dubiously, hesitating a moment, then drawing up chair and sitting down.] I . . . I do not understand.

LORETTA. [Wailing.] I am so unhappy!

NED. [Inquisitorially.] Why unhappy?

LORETTA. Because . . . he . . . he wants to marry me.

NED. [His face brightening instantly, leaning forward and laying a hand soothingly on hers.] That should not make any girl unhappy. Because you don't love him is no reason--[Abruptly breaking off.] Of course you don't love him? [LORETTA shakes her head and shoulders vigorously.] What?

LORETTA. [Explosively.] No, I don't love Billy! I don't want to love Billy!

NED. [With confidence.] Because you don't love him is no reason that you should be unhappy just because he has proposed to you.

LORETTA. [Sobbing.] That's the trouble. I wish I did love him. Oh, I wish I were dead.

NED. [Growing complacent.] Now my dear child, you are worrying yourself over trifles. [His second hand joins the first in holding her hands.] Women do it every day. Because you have changed your mind, or did not know you mind, because you have--to use an unnecessarily harsh word--jilted a man--

LORETTA. [Interrupting, raising her head and looking at him.] Jilted? Oh Ned, if that were a all!

NED. [Hollow voice.] All!

[NED's hands slowly retreat from hers. He opens his mouth as though to speak further, then changes his mind and remains silent.]

LORETTA. [Protestingly.] But I don't want to marry him!

NED. Then I shouldn't.

LORETTA. But I ought to marry him.

NED. Ought to marry him? [LORETTA nods.] That is a strong word.

LORETTA. [Nodding.] I know it is. [Her lips are trembling, but she strives for control and manages to speak more calmly.] I am a wicked woman. A terrible wicked woman. No one knows how wicked I am . . . except Billy.

NED. [Starting, looking at her queerly.] He . . . Billy knows? [LORETTA nods. He debates with himself a moment.] Tell me about it. You must tell me all of it.

LORETTA. [Faintly, as though about to weep again.] All of it?

NED. [Firmly.] Yes, all of it.

LORETTA. [Haltingly.] And . . . will . . . you . . . ever . . . forgive . . . me?

NED. [Drawing a long, breath, desperately.] Yes, I'll forgive you. Go ahead.

LORETTA. There was no one to tell me. We were with each other so much. I did not know anything of the world . . . then. [Pauses.]

NED. [Impatiently.] Go on.

LORETTA. If I had only known. [Pauses.]

NED. [Biting his lip and clenching his hands.] Yes, yes. Go on.

LORETTA. We were together almost every evening.

NED. [Savagely.] Billy?

LORETTA. Yes, of course, Billy. We were with each other so much . . . If I had only known . . . There was no one to tell me . . . I was so young . . . [Breaks down crying.]

NED. [Leaping to his feet, explosively.] The scoundrel!

LORETTA. [Lifting her head.] Billy is not a scoundrel . . . He . . . he . . . is a good man.

NED. [Sarcastically.] I suppose you'll be telling me next that it was all your fault. [LORETTA nods.] What!

LORETTA. [Steadily.] It was all my fault. I should never have let him. I was to blame.

NED. [Paces up and down for a minute, stops in front of her, and speaks with resignation.] All right. I don't blame you in the least, Loretta. And you have been very honest. It is . . . er . . . commendable. But Billy is right, and you are wrong. You must get married.

LORETTA. [In dim, far-away voice.] To Billy?

NED. Yes, to Billy. I'll see to it. Where does he live? I'll make him. If he won't I'll . . . I'll shoot him!

LORETTA. [Crying out with alarm.] Oh, Ned, you won't do that?

NED. [Sternly.] I shall.

LORETTA. But I don't want to marry Billy.

NED. [Sternly.] You must. And Billy must. Do you understand? It is the only thing.

LORETTA. That's what Billy said.

NED. [Triumphantly.] You see, I am right.

LORETTA. And if . . . if I don't marry him . . . there will be . . . scandal?

NED. [Calmly.] Yes, there will be scandal.

LORETTA. That's what Billy said. Oh, I am so unhappy!

[LORETTA breaks down into violent weeping.]

[NED paces grimly up and down, now and again fiercely twisting his moustache.]

LORETTA. [Face buried, sobbing and crying all the time.]

I don't want to leave Daisy! I don't want to leave Daisy! What shall I do? What shall I do? How was I to know? He didn't tell me. Nobody else ever kissed me. [NED stops curiously to listen. As he listens his face brightens.] I never dreamed a kiss could be so terrible . . . until . . . until he told me. He only told me this morning.

NED. [Abruptly.] Is that what you are crying about?

LORETTA. [Reluctantly.] N-no.

NED. [In hopeless voice, the brightness gone out of his face, about to begin pacing again.] Then what are you crying about?

LORETTA. Because you said I had to marry Billy. I don't want to marry Billy. I don't want to leave Daisy. I don't know what I want. I wish I were dead.

NED. [Nerving himself for another effort.] Now look here, Loretta, be sensible. What is this about kisses? You haven't told me everything after all.

LORETTA. I . . . I don't want to tell you everything.

NED. [Imperatively.] You must.

LORETTA. [Surrendering.] Well, then . . . must I?

NED. You must.

LORETTA. [Floundering.] He . . . I . . . we . . . I let him, and he kissed me.

NED. [Desperately, controlling himself.] Go on.

LORETTA. He says eight, but I can't think of more than five times.

NED. Yes, go on.

LORETTA. That's all.

NED. [With vast incredulity.] All?

LORETTA. [Puzzled.] All?

NED. [Awkwardly.] I mean . . . er . . . nothing worse?

LORETTA. [Puzzled.] Worse? As though there could be. Billy said--

NED. [Interrupting.] When?

LORETTA. This afternoon. Just now. Billy said that my . . . our . . . our . . . our kisses were terrible if we didn't get married.

NED. What else did he say?

LORETTA. He said that when a woman permitted a man to kiss her she always married him. That it was awful if she didn't. It was the custom, he said; and I say it is a bad, wicked custom, and it has broken my heart. I shall never be happy again. I know I am terrible, but I can't help it. I must have been born wicked.

NED. [Absent-mindedly bringing out a cigarette and striking a match.] Do you mind if I smoke? [Coming to himself again, and flinging away match and cigarette.] I beg your pardon. I don't want to smoke. I didn't mean that at all. What I mean is . . . [He bends over LORETTA, catches her hands in his, then sits on arm of chair, softly puts one arm around her, and is about to kiss her.]

LORETTA. [With horror, repulsing him.] No! No!

NED. [Surprised.] What's the matter?

LORETTA. [Agitatedly.] Would you make me a wickeder woman than I am?

NED. A kiss?

LORETTA. There will be another scandal. That would make two scandals.

NED. To kiss the woman I love . . . a scandal?

LORETTA. Billy loves me, and he said so.

NED. Billy is a joker . . . or else he is as innocent as you.

LORETTA. But you said so yourself.

NED. [Taken aback.] I?

LORETTA. Yes, you said it yourself, with your own lips, not ten minutes ago. I shall never believe you again.

NED. [Masterfully putting arm around her and drawing her toward him.] And I am a joker, too, and a very wicked man. Nevertheless, you must trust me. There will be nothing wrong.

LORETTA. [Preparing to yield.] And no . . . scandal?

NED. Scandal fiddlesticks. Loretta, I want you to be my wife. [He waits anxiously.]

[JACK HEMINGWAY, in fishing costume, appears in doorway to right and looks on.]

NED. You might say something.

LORETTA. I will . . . if . . .

[ALICE HEMINGWAY appears in doorway to left and looks on.]

NED. [In suspense.] Yes, go on.

LORETTA. If I don't have to marry Billy.

NED. [Almost shouting.] You can't marry both of us!

LORETTA. [Sadly, repulsing him with her hands.] Then, Ned, I cannot marry you.

NED. [Dumbfounded.] W-what?

LORETTA. [Sadly.] Because I can't marry both of you.

NED. Bosh and nonsense!

LORETTA. I'd like to marry you, but . . .

NED. There is nothing to prevent you.

LORETTA. [With sad conviction.] Oh, yes, there is. You said yourself that I had to marry Billy. You said you would s-s-shoot him if he didn't.

NED. [Drawing her toward him.] Nevertheless . . .

LORETTA. [Slightly holding him off.] And it isn't the custom . . . what . . . Billy said?

NED. No, it isn't the custom. Now, Loretta, will you marry me?

LORETTA. [Pouting demurely.] Don't be angry with me, Ned. [He gathers her into his arms and kisses her. She partially frees herself, gasping.] I wish it were the custom, because now I'd have to marry you, Ned, wouldn't I?

[NED and LORETTA kiss a second time and profoundly.]

[JACK HEMINGWAY chuckles.]

[NED and LORETTA, startled, but still in each other's arms, look around. NED looks sillily at ALICE HEMINGWAY. LORETTA looks at JACK HEMINGWAY.]

LORETTA. I don't care.

CURTAIN

THE BIRTH MARK SKETCH BY JACK LONDON written for Robert and Julia Fitzsimmons

SCENE--One of the club rooms of the West Bay Athletic Club. Near centre front is a large table covered with newspapers and magazines. At left a punching-bag apparatus. At right, against wall, a desk, on which rests a desk-telephone. Door at rear toward left. On walls are framed pictures of pugilists, conspicuous among which is one of Robert Fitzsimmons. Appropriate furnishings, etc., such as foils, clubs, dumb-bells and trophies.

[Enter MAUD SYLVESTER.]

[She is dressed as a man, in evening clothes, preferably a Tuxedo. In her hand is a card, and under her arm a paper-wrapped parcel. She peeps about curiously and advances to table. She is timorous and excited, elated and at the same time frightened. Her eyes are dancing with excitement.]

MAUD. [Pausing by table.] Not a soul saw me. I wonder where everybody is. And that big brother of mine said I could not get in. [She reads back of card.] "Here is my card, Maudie. If you can use it, go ahead. But you will never get inside the door. I consider my bet as good as won." [Looking up, triumphantly.] You do, do you? Oh, if you could see your little sister now. Here she is, inside. [Pauses, and looks about.] So this is the West Bay Athletic Club. No women allowed. Well, here I am, if I don't look like one. [Stretches out one leg and then the other, and looks at them. Leaving card and parcel on table, she struts around like a man, looks at pictures of pugilists on walls, reading aloud their names and making appropriate remarks. But she stops before the portrait of Fitzsimmons and reads aloud.] "Robert Fitzsimmons, the greatest warrior of them all." [Clasps hands, and looking up at portrait murmurs.] Oh, you dear!

[Continues strutting around, imitating what she considers are a man's stride and swagger, returns to table and proceeds to unwrap parcel.] Well, I'll go out like a girl, if I did come in like a man. [Drops wrapping paper on table and holds up a woman's long automobile cloak and a motor bonnet. Is suddenly startled by sound of approaching footsteps and glances in a frightened way toward door.] Mercy! Here comes somebody now! [Glances about her in alarm, drops cloak and bonnet on floor close to table, seizes a handful of newspapers, and runs to large leather chair to right of table, where she seats herself hurriedly. One paper she holds up before her, hiding her face as she pretends to read. Unfortunately the paper is upside down. The other papers lie on her lap.]

[Enter ROBERT FITZSIMMONS.]

[He looks about, advances to table, takes out cigarette case and is about to select one, when he notices motor cloak and bonnet on floor. He lays cigarette case on table and picks them up. They strike him as profoundly curious things to be in a club room. He looks at MAUD, then sees card on table. He picks it up and reach it to himself, then looks at her with comprehension. Hidden by her newspaper, she sees nothing. He looks at card again and reads and speaks in an aside.]

FITZSIMMONS. "Maudie. John H. Sylvester." That must be Jack Sylvester's sister Maud. [FITZSIMMONS shows by his expression that he is going to play a joke. Tossing cloak and bonnet under the table he places card in his vest pocket, selects a chair, sits down, and looks at MAUD. He notes paper is upside down, is hugely tickled, and laughs silently.] Hello! [Newspaper is agitated by slight tremor. He speaks more loudly.] Hello! [Newspaper shakes badly. He speaks very loudly.] Hello!

MAUD. [Peeping at him over top of paper and speaking hesitatingly.] H-h-hello!

FITZSIMMONS. [Gruffly.] You are a queer one, reading a paper upside down.

MAUD. [Lowering newspaper and trying to appear at ease.] It's quite a trick, isn't it? I often practise it. I'm real clever at it, you know.

FITZSIMMONS. [Grunts, then adds.] Seems to me I have seen you before.

MAUD. [Glancing quickly from his face to portrait and back again.] Yes, and I know you--You are Robert Fitzsimmons.

FITZSIMMONS. I thought I knew you.

MAUD. Yes, it was out in San Francisco. My people still live there. I'm just--ahem--doing New York.

FITZSIMMONS. But I don't quite remember the name.

MAUD. Jones--Harry Jones.

FITZSIMMONS. [Hugely delighted, leaping from chair and striding over to her.] Sure. [Slaps her resoundingly on shoulder.]

[She is nearly crushed by the weight of the blow, and at the same time shocked. She scrambles to her feet.]

FITZSIMMONS. Glad to see you, Harry. [He wrings her hand, so that it hurts.] Glad to see you again, Harry. [He continues wringing her hand and pumping her arm.]

MAUD. [Struggling to withdraw her hand and finally succeeding. Her voice is rather faint.] Ye-es, er . . . Bob . . . er . . . glad to see you again. [She looks ruefully at her bruised fingers and sinks into chair. Then, recollecting her part, she crosses her legs in a mannish way.]

FITZSIMMONS. [Crossing to desk at right, against which he leans, facing her.] You were a wild young rascal in those San Francisco days. [Chuckling.] Lord, Lord, how it all comes back to me.

MAUD. [Boastfully.] I was wild--some.

FITZSIMMONS. [Grinning.] I should say! Remember that night I put you to bed?

MAUD. [Forgetting herself, indignantly.] Sir!

FITZSIMMONS. You were . . . er . . . drunk.

MAUD. I never was!

FITZSIMMONS. Surely you haven't forgotten that night! You began with dropping champagne bottles out of the club windows on the heads of the people on the sidewalk, and you wound up by assaulting a cabman. And let me tell you I saved you from a good licking right there, and squared it with the police. Don't you remember?

MAUD. [Nodding hesitatingly.] Yes, it is beginning to come back to me. I was a bit tight that night.

FITZSIMMONS. [Exultantly.] A bit tight! Why, before I could get you to bed you insisted on telling me the story of your life.

MAUD. Did I? I don't remember that.

FITZSIMMONS. I should say not. You were past remembering anything by that time. You had your arms around my neck--

MAUD. [Interrupting.] Oh!

FITZSIMMONS. And you kept repeating over and over, "Bob, dear Bob."

MAUD. [Springing to her feet.] Oh! I never did! [Recollecting herself.] Perhaps I must have. I was a trifle wild in those days, I admit. But I'm wise now. I've sowed my wild oats and steadied down.

FITZSIMMONS. I'm glad to hear that, Harry. You were tearing off a pretty fast pace in those days. [Pause, in which MAUD nods.] Still punch the bag?

MAUD. [In quick alarm, glancing at punching bag.] No, I've got out of the hang of it.

FITZSIMMONS. [Reproachfully.] You haven't forgotten that right-and-left, arm, elbow and shoulder movement I taught you?

MAUD. [With hesitation.] N-o-o.

FITZSIMMONS. [Moving toward bag to left.] Then, come on.

MAUD. [Rising reluctantly and following.] I'd rather see you punch the bag. I'd just love to.

FITZSIMMONS. I will, afterward. You go to it first.

MAUD. [Eyeing the bag in alarm.] No; you. I'm out of practice.

FITZSIMMONS. [Looking at her sharply.] How many drinks have you had to- night?

MAUD. Not a one. I don't drink--that is--er--only occasionally.

FITZSIMMONS. [Indicating bag.] Then go to it.

MAUD. No; I tell you I am out of practice. I've forgotten it all. You see, I made a discovery.

[Pauses.]

FITZSIMMONS. Yes?

MAUD. I--I--you remember what a light voice I always had--almost soprano?

[FITZSIMMONS nods.]

MAUD. Well, I discovered it was a perfect falsetto.

[FITZSIMMONS nods.]

MAUD. I've been practising it ever since. Experts, in another room, would swear it was a woman's voice. So would you, if you turned your back and I sang.

FITZSIMMONS. [Who has been laughing incredulously, now becomes suspicious.] Look here, kid, I think you are an impostor. You are not Harry Jones at all.

MAUD. I am, too.

FITZSIMMONS. I don't believe it. He was heavier than you.

MAUD. I had the fever last summer and lost a lot of weight.

FITZSIMMONS. You are the Harry Jones that got sousesd and had to be put to bed?

MAUD. Y-e-s.

FITZSIMMONS. There is one thing I remember very distinctly. Harry Jones had a birth mark on his knee. [He looks at her legs searchingly.]

MAUD. [Embarrassed, then resolving to carry it out.] Yes, right here. [She advances right leg and touches it.]

FITZSIMMONS. [Triumphantly.] Wrong. It was the other knee.

MAUD. I ought to know.

FITZSIMMONS. You haven't any birth mark at all.

MAUD. I have, too.

FITZSIMMONS. [Suddenly springing to her and attempting to seize her leg.] Then we'll prove it. Let me see.

MAUD. [In a panic backs away from him and resists his attempts, until grinning in an aside to the audience, he gives over. She, in an aside to audience.] Fancy his wanting to see my birth mark.

FITZSIMMONS. [Bullying.] Then take a go at the bag. [She shakes her head.] You're not Harry Jones.

MAUD. [Approaching punching bag.] I am, too.

FITZSIMMONS. Then hit it.

MAUD. [Resolving to attempt it, hits bag several nice blows, and then is struck on the nose by it.] Oh!

[Recovering herself and rubbing her nose.] I told you I was out of practice. You punch the bag, Bob.

FITZSIMMONS. I will, if you will show me what you can do with that wonderful soprano voice of yours.

MAUD. I don't dare. Everybody would think there was a woman in the club.

FITZSIMMONS. [Shaking his head.] No, they won't. They've all gone to the fight. There's not a soul in the building.

MAUD. [Alarmed, in a weak voice.] Not--a--soul--in--the building?

FITZSIMMONS. Not a soul. Only you and I.

MAUD. [Starting hurriedly toward door.] Then I must go.

FITZSIMMONS. What's your hurry? Sing.

MAUD. [Turning back with new resolve.] Let me see you punch the bag,--er--Bob.

FITZSIMMONS. You sing first.

MAUD. No; you punch first.

FITZSIMMONS. I don't believe you are Harry--

MAUD. [Hastily.] All right, I'll sing. You sit down over there and turn your back.

[FITZSIMMONS obeys.]

[MAUD walks over to the table toward right. She is about to sing, when she notices FITZSIMMONS' cigarette case, picks it up, and in an aside reads his name on it and speaks.]

MAUD. "Robert Fitzsimmons." That will prove to my brother that I have been here.

FITZSIMMONS. Hurry up.

[MAUD hastily puts cigarette case in her pocket and begins to sing.]

SONG

[During the song FITZSIMMONS turns his head slowly and looks at her with growing admiration.]

MAUD. How did you like it?

FITZSIMMONS. [Gruffly.] Rotten. Anybody could tell it was a boy's voice--

MAUD. Oh!

FITZSIMMONS. It is rough and coarse and it cracked on every high note.

MAUD. Oh! Oh!

[Recollecting herself and shrugging her shoulders.] Oh, very well. Now let's see if you can do any better with the bag.

[FITZSIMMONS takes off coat and gives exhibition.]

[MAUD looks on in an ecstasy of admiration.]

MAUD. [As he finishes.] Beautiful! Beautiful!

[FITZSIMMONS puts on coat and goes over and sits down near table.] Nothing like the bag to limber one up. I feel like a fighting cock. Harry, let's go out on a toot, you and I.

MAUD. Wh-a-a-t?

FITZSIMMONS. A toot. You know--one of those rip-snorting nights you used to make.

MAUD. [Emphatically, as she picks up newspapers from leather chair, sits down, and places them on her lap.] I'll do nothing of the sort. I've--I've reformed.

FITZSIMMONS. You used to joy-ride like the very devil.

MAUD. I know it.

FITZSIMMONS. And you always had a pretty girl or two along.

MAUD. [Boastfully, in mannish, fashion.] Oh, I still have my fling. Do you know any--well,--er,--nice girls?

FITZSIMMONS. Sure.

MAUD. Put me wise.

FITZSIMMONS. Sure. You know Jack Sylvester?

MAUD. [Forgetting herself.] He's my brother--

FITZSIMMONS. [Exploding.] What!

MAUD.--In-law's first cousin.

FITZSIMMONS. Oh!

MAUD. So you see I don't know him very well. I only met him once--at the club. We had a drink together.

FITZSIMMONS. Then you don't know his sister?

MAUD. [Starting.] His sister? I--I didn't know he had a sister.

FITZSIMMONS. [Enthusiastically.] She's a peach. A queen. A little bit of all right. A--a loo-loo.

MAUD. [Flattered.] She is, is she?

FITZSIMMONS. She's a scream. You ought to get acquainted with her.

MAUD. [Slyly.] You know her, then?

FITZSIMMONS. You bet.

MAUD. [Aside.] Oh, ho! [To FITZSIMMONS.] Know her very well?

FITZSIMMONS. I've taken her out more times than I can remember. You'll like her, I'm sure.

MAUD. Thanks. Tell me some more about her.

FITZSIMMONS. She dresses a bit loud. But you won't mind that. And whatever you do, don't take her to eat.

MAUD. [Hiding her chagrin.] Why not?

FITZSIMMONS. I never saw such an appetite--

MAUD. Oh!

FITZSIMMONS. It's fair sickening. She must have a tapeworm. And she thinks she can sing.

MAUD. Yes?

FITZSIMMONS. Rotten. You can do better yourself, and that's not saying much. She's a nice girl, really she is, but she is the black sheep of the family. Funny, isn't it?

MAUD. [Weak voice.] Yes, funny.

FITZSIMMONS. Her brother Jack is all right. But he can't do anything with her. She's a--a--

MAUD. [Grimly.] Yes. Go on.

FITZSIMMONS. A holy terror. She ought to be in a reform school.

MAUD. [Springing to her feet and slamming newspapers in his face.] Oh! Oh! Oh! You liar! She isn't anything of the sort!

FITZSIMMONS. [Recovering from the onslaught and making believe he is angry, advancing threateningly on her.] Now I'm going to put a head on you. You young hoodlum.

MAUD. [All alarm and contrition, backing away from him.] Don't! Please don't! I'm sorry! I apologise. I--I beg your pardon, Bob. Only I don't like to hear girls talked about that way, even--even if it is true. And you ought to know.

FITZSIMMONS. [Subsiding and resuming seat.] You've changed a lot, I must say.

MAUD. [Sitting down in leather chair.] I told you I'd reformed. Let us talk about something else. Why is it girls like prize-fighters? I should think--ahem--I mean it seems to me that girls would think prize- fighters horrid.

FITZSIMMONS. They are men.

MAUD. But there is so much crookedness in the game. One hears about it all the time.

FITZSIMMONS. There are crooked men in every business and profession. The best fighters are not crooked.

MAUD. I--er--I thought they all faked fights when there was enough in it.

FITZSIMMONS. Not the best ones.

MAUD. Did you--er--ever fake a fight?

FITZSIMMONS. [Looking at her sharply, then speaking solemnly.] Yes. Once.

MAUD. [Shocked, speaking sadly.] And I always heard of you and thought of you as the one clean champion who never faked.

FITZSIMMONS. [Gently and seriously.] Let me tell you about it. It was down in Australia. I had just begun to fight my way up. It was with old Bill Hobart out at Rushcutters Bay. I threw the fight to him.

MAUD. [Repelled, disgusted.] Oh! I could not have believed it of you.

FITZSIMMONS. Let me tell you about it. Bill was an old fighter. Not an old man, you know, but he'd been in the fighting game a long time. He was about thirty-eight and a gamer man never entered the ring. But he was in hard luck. Younger fighters were coming up, and he was being crowded out. At that time it wasn't often he got a fight and the purses were small. Besides it was a drought year in Australia. You don't know what that means. It means that the rangers are starved. It means that the sheep are starved and die by the millions. It means that there is no money and no work, and that the men and women and kiddies starve.

Bill Hobart had a missus and three kids and at the time of his fight with me they were all starving. They did not have enough to eat. Do you understand? They did not have enough to eat. And Bill did not have enough to eat. He trained on an empty stomach, which is no way to train you'll admit. During that drought year there was little enough money in the ring, but he had failed to get any fights. He had worked at long- shoring, ditch-digging, coal-shovelling--anything, to keep the life in the missus and the kiddies. The trouble was the jobs didn't hold out. And there he was, matched to fight with me, behind in his rent, a tough old chopping-block, but weak from lack of food. If he did not win the fight, the landlord was going to put them into the street.

MAUD. But why would you want to fight with him in such weak condition?

FITZSIMMONS. I did not know. I did not learn till at the ringside just before the fight. It was in the dressing rooms, waiting our turn to go on. Bill came out of his room, ready for the ring. "Bill," I said--in fun, you know. "Bill, I've got to do you to-night." He said nothing, but he looked at me with the saddest and most pitiful face I have ever seen. He went back into his dressing room and sat down.

"Poor Bill!" one of my seconds said. "He's been fair starving these last weeks. And I've got it straight, the landlord chucks him out if he loses to-night."

Then the call came and we went into the ring. Bill was desperate. He fought like a tiger, a madman. He was fair crazy. He was fighting for more than I was fighting for. I was a rising fighter, and I was fighting for the money and the recognition. But Bill was fighting for life--for the life of his loved ones.

Well, condition told. The strength went out of him, and I was fresh as a daisy. "What's the matter, Bill?" I said to him in a clinch. "You're weak." "I ain't had a bit to eat this day," he answered. That was all.

By the seventh round he was about all in, hanging on and panting and sobbing for breath in the clinches, and I knew I could put him out any time. I drew back my right for the short-arm jab that would do the business. He knew it was coming, and he was powerless to prevent it.

"For the love of God, Bob," he said; and--[Pause.]

MAUD. Yes? Yes?

FITZSIMMONS. I held back the blow. We were in a clinch.

"For the love of God, Bob," he said again, "the misses and the kiddies!"

And right there I saw and knew it all. I saw the hungry children asleep, and the missus sitting up and waiting for Bill to come home, waiting to know whether they were to have food to eat or be thrown out in the street.

"Bill," I said, in the next clinch, so low only he could hear. "Bill, remember the La Blanche swing. Give it to me, hard."

We broke away, and he was tottering and groggy. He staggered away and started to whirl the swing. I saw it coming. I made believe I didn't and started after him in a rush. Biff! It caught me on the jaw, and I went down. I was young and strong. I could eat punishment. I could have got up the first second. But I lay there and let them count me out. And making believe I was still dazed, I let them carry me to my corner and work to bring me to. [Pause.]

Well, I faked that fight.

MAUD. [Springing to him and shaking his hand.] Thank God! Oh! You are a man! A--a--a hero!

FITZSIMMONS. [Dryly, feeling in his pocket.] Let's have a smoke. [He fails to find cigarette case.]

MAUD. I can't tell you how glad I am you told me that.

FITZSIMMONS. [Gruffly.] Forget it. [He looks on table, and fails to find cigarette case. Looks at her suspiciously, then crosses to desk at right and reaches for telephone.]

MAUD. [Curiously.] What are you going to do?

FITZSIMMONS. Call the police.

MAUD. What for?

FITZSIMMONS. For you.

MAUD. For me?

FITZSIMMONS. You are not Harry Jones. And not only are you an impostor, but you are a thief.

MAUD. [Indignantly.] How dare you?

FITZSIMMONS. You have stolen my cigarette case.

MAUD. [Remembering and taken aback, pulls out cigarette case.] Here it is.

FITZSIMMONS. Too late. It won't save you. This club must be kept respectable. Thieves cannot be tolerated.

MAUD. [Growing alarm.] But you won't have me arrested?

FITZSIMMONS. I certainly will.

MAUD. [Pleadingly.] Please! Please!

FITZSIMMONS. [Obdurately.] I see no reason why I should not.

MAUD. [Hurriedly, in a panic.] I'll give you a reason--a--a good one. I--I--am not Harry Jones.

FITZSIMMONS. [Grimly.] A good reason in itself to call in the police.

MAUD. That isn't the reason. I'm--a--Oh! I'm so ashamed.

FITZSIMMONS. [Sternly.] I should say you ought to be. [Reaches for telephone receiver.]

MAUD. [In rush of desperation.] Stop! I'm a--I'm a--a girl. There! [Sinks down in chair, burying her face in her hands.]

[FITZSIMMONS, hanging up receiver, grunts.]

[MAUD removes hands and looks at him indignantly. As she speaks her indignation grows.]

MAUD. I only wanted your cigarette case to prove to my brother that I had been here. I--I'm Maud Sylvester, and you never took me out once. And I'm not a black sheep. And I don't dress loudly, and I haven't a--a tapeworm.

FITZSIMMONS. [Grinning and pulling out card from vest pocket.] I knew you were Miss Sylvester all the time.

MAUD. Oh! You brute! I'll never speak to you again.

FITZSIMMONS. [Gently.] You'll let me see you safely out of here.

MAUD. [Relenting.] Ye-e-s. [She rises, crosses to table, and is about to stoop for motor cloak and bonnet, but he forestall her, holds cloak and helps her into it.] Thank you. [She takes off wig, fluffs her own hair becomingly, and puts on bonnet, looking every inch a pretty young girl, ready for an automobile ride.]

FITZSIMMONS. [Who, all the time, watching her transformation, has been growing bashful, now handing her the cigarette case.] Here's the cigarette case. You may k-k-keep it.

MAUD. [Looking at him, hesitates, then takes it.] I thank you--er--Bob. I shall treasure it all my life. [He is very embarrassed.] Why, I do believe you're bashful. What is the matter?

FITZSIMMONS. [Stammering.] Why--I--you--You are a girl--and--a--a-- deuced pretty one.

MAUD. [Taking his arm, ready to start for door.] But you knew it all along.

FITZSIMMONS. But it's somehow different now when you've got your girl's clothes on.

MAUD. But you weren't a bit bashful--or nice, when--you--you--[Blurting it out.] Were so anxious about birth marks.

[They start to make exit.]

CURTAIN

******* This file should be named 1669.txt or 1669.zip *******

This and all associated files of various formats will be found in:
 http://www.gutenberg.org/dirs/1/6/6/1669

Updated editions will replace the previous one--the old editions will be renamed.

Creating the works from public domain print editions means that no one owns a United States copyright in these works, so the Foundation (and you!) can copy and distribute it in the United States without permission and without paying copyright royalties. Special rules, set forth in the General Terms of Use part of this license, apply to copying and distributing Project Gutenberg-tm electronic works to protect the PROJECT GUTENBERG-tm concept and trademark. Project Gutenberg is a registered trademark, and may not be used if you charge for the eBooks, unless you receive specific permission. If you do not charge anything for copies of this eBook, complying with the rules is very easy. You may use this eBook for nearly any purpose such as creation of derivative works, reports, performances and research. They may be modified and printed and given away--you may do practically ANYTHING with public domain eBooks. Redistribution is subject to the trademark license, especially commercial redistribution.

*** START: FULL LICENSE ***

THE FULL PROJECT GUTENBERG LICENSE PLEASE READ THIS BEFORE YOU DISTRIBUTE OR USE THIS WORK

To protect the Project Gutenberg-tm mission of promoting the free distribution of electronic works, by using or distributing this work (or any other work associated in any way with the phrase "Project Gutenberg"), you agree to comply with all the terms of the Full Project Gutenberg-tm License (available with this file or online at http://gutenberg.net/license).

Section 1. General Terms of Use and Redistributing Project Gutenberg-tm electronic works

1.A. By reading or using any part of this Project Gutenberg-tm electronic work, you indicate that you have read, understand, agree to and accept all the terms of this license and intellectual property (trademark/copyright) agreement. If you do not agree to abide by all the terms of this agreement, you must cease using and return or destroy all copies of Project Gutenberg-tm electronic works in your possession. If you paid a fee for obtaining a copy of or access to a Project Gutenberg-tm electronic work and you do not agree to be bound by the terms of this agreement, you may obtain a refund from the person or entity to whom you paid the fee as set forth in paragraph 1.E.8.

1.B. "Project Gutenberg" is a registered trademark. It may only be used on or associated in any way with an electronic work by people who agree to be bound by the terms of this agreement. There are a few things that you can do with most Project Gutenberg-tm electronic works even without complying with the full terms of this agreement. See paragraph 1.C below. There are a lot of things you can do with Project Gutenberg-tm electronic works if you follow the terms of this agreement and help preserve free future access to Project Gutenberg-tm electronic works. See paragraph 1.E below.

1.C. The Project Gutenberg Literary Archive Foundation ("the Foundation" or PGLAF), owns a compilation copyright in the collection of Project Gutenberg-tm electronic works. Nearly all the individual works in the collection are in the public domain in the United States. If an individual work is in the public domain in the United States and you are located in the United States, we do not claim a right to prevent you from copying, distributing, performing, displaying or creating derivative works based on the work as long as all references to Project Gutenberg are removed. Of course, we hope that you will support the Project Gutenberg-tm mission of promoting free access to electronic works by freely sharing Project Gutenberg-tm works in compliance with the terms of this agreement for keeping the Project Gutenberg-tm name associated with the work. You can easily comply with the terms of this agreement by keeping this work in the same format with its attached full Project Gutenberg-tm License when you share it without charge with others.

1.D. The copyright laws of the place where you are located also govern what you can do with this work. Copyright laws in most countries are in a constant state of change. If you are outside the United States, check the laws of your country in addition to the terms of this agreement before downloading, copying, displaying, performing, distributing or creating derivative works based on this work or any other Project Gutenberg-tm work. The Foundation makes no representations concerning the copyright status of any work in any country outside the United States.

1.E. Unless you have removed all references to Project Gutenberg:

1.E.1. The following sentence, with active links to, or other immediate access to, the full Project Gutenberg-tm License must appear prominently whenever any copy of a Project Gutenberg-tm work (any work on which the phrase "Project Gutenberg" appears, or with which the phrase "Project Gutenberg" is associated) is accessed, displayed, performed, viewed, copied or distributed:

This eBook is for the use of anyone anywhere at no cost and with almost no restrictions whatsoever. You may copy it, give it away or re-use it under the terms of the Project Gutenberg License included with this eBook or online at www.gutenberg.net

1.E.2. If an individual Project Gutenberg-tm electronic work is derived from the public domain (does not contain a notice indicating that it is posted with permission of the copyright holder), the work can be copied and distributed to anyone in the United States without paying any fees or charges. If you are redistributing or providing access to a work with the phrase "Project Gutenberg" associated with or appearing on the work, you must comply either with the requirements of paragraphs 1.E.1 through 1.E.7 or obtain permission for the use of the work and the Project Gutenberg-tm trademark as set forth in paragraphs 1.E.8 or 1.E.9.

1.E.3. If an individual Project Gutenberg-tm electronic work is posted with the permission of the copyright holder, your use and distribution must comply with both paragraphs 1.E.1 through 1.E.7 and any additional terms imposed by the copyright holder. Additional terms will be linked to the Project Gutenberg-tm License for all works posted with the permission of the copyright holder found at the beginning of this work.

1.E.4. Do not unlink or detach or remove the full Project Gutenberg-tm License terms from this work, or any files containing a part of this work or any other work associated with Project Gutenberg-tm.

1.E.5. Do not copy, display, perform, distribute or redistribute this electronic work, or any part of this electronic work, without prominently displaying the sentence set forth in paragraph 1.E.1 with active links or immediate access to the full terms of the Project Gutenberg-tm License.

1.E.6. You may convert to and distribute this work in any binary, compressed, marked up, nonproprietary or proprietary form, including any word processing or hypertext form. However, if you provide access to or distribute copies of a Project Gutenberg-tm work in a format other than "Plain Vanilla ASCII" or other format used in the official version posted on the official Project Gutenberg-tm web site (www.gutenberg.net), you must, at no additional cost, fee or expense to the user, provide a copy, a means of exporting a copy, or a means of obtaining a copy upon request, of the work in its original "Plain Vanilla ASCII" or other form. Any alternate format must include the full Project Gutenberg-tm License as specified in paragraph 1.E.1.

1.E.7. Do not charge a fee for access to, viewing, displaying, performing, copying or distributing any Project Gutenberg-tm works unless you comply with paragraph 1.E.8 or 1.E.9.

1.E.8. You may charge a reasonable fee for copies of or providing access to or distributing Project Gutenberg-tm electronic works provided that

- You pay a royalty fee of 20% of the gross profits you derive from the use of Project Gutenberg-tm works calculated using the method you already use to calculate your applicable taxes. The fee is owed to the owner of the Project Gutenberg-tm trademark, but he has agreed to donate royalties under this paragraph to the Project Gutenberg Literary Archive Foundation. Royalty payments must be paid within 60 days following each date on which you prepare (or are legally required to prepare) your periodic tax returns. Royalty payments should be clearly marked as such and sent to the Project Gutenberg Literary Archive Foundation at the address specified in Section 4, "Information about donations to the Project Gutenberg Literary Archive

Foundation."

- You provide a full refund of any money paid by a user who notifies you in writing (or by e-mail) within 30 days of receipt that s/he does not agree to the terms of the full Project Gutenberg-tm License. You must require such a user to return or destroy all copies of the works possessed in a physical medium and discontinue all use of and all access to other copies of Project Gutenberg-tm works.

- You provide, in accordance with paragraph 1.F.3, a full refund of any money paid for a work or a replacement copy, if a defect in the electronic work is discovered and reported to you within 90 days of receipt of the work.

- You comply with all other terms of this agreement for free distribution of Project Gutenberg-tm works.

1.E.9. If you wish to charge a fee or distribute a Project Gutenberg-tm electronic work or group of works on different terms than are set forth in this agreement, you must obtain permission in writing from both the Project Gutenberg Literary Archive Foundation and Michael Hart, the owner of the Project Gutenberg-tm trademark. Contact the Foundation as set forth in Section 3 below.

1.F.

1.F.1. Project Gutenberg volunteers and employees expend considerable effort to identify, do copyright research on, transcribe and proofread public domain works in creating the Project Gutenberg-tm collection. Despite these efforts, Project Gutenberg-tm electronic works, and the medium on which they may be stored, may contain "Defects," such as, but not limited to, incomplete, inaccurate or corrupt data, transcription errors, a copyright or other intellectual property infringement, a defective or damaged disk or other medium, a computer virus, or computer codes that damage or cannot be read by your equipment.

1.F.2. LIMITED WARRANTY, DISCLAIMER OF DAMAGES - Except for the "Right of Replacement or Refund" described in paragraph 1.F.3, the Project Gutenberg Literary Archive Foundation, the owner of the Project Gutenberg-tm trademark, and any other party distributing a Project Gutenberg-tm electronic work under this agreement, disclaim all liability to you for damages, costs and expenses, including legal fees. YOU AGREE THAT YOU HAVE NO REMEDIES FOR NEGLIGENCE, STRICT LIABILITY, BREACH OF WARRANTY OR BREACH OF CONTRACT EXCEPT THOSE PROVIDED IN PARAGRAPH F3. YOU AGREE THAT THE FOUNDATION, THE TRADEMARK OWNER, AND ANY DISTRIBUTOR UNDER THIS AGREEMENT WILL NOT BE LIABLE TO YOU FOR ACTUAL, DIRECT, INDIRECT, CONSEQUENTIAL, PUNITIVE OR INCIDENTAL DAMAGES EVEN IF YOU GIVE NOTICE OF THE POSSIBILITY OF SUCH DAMAGE.

1.F.3. LIMITED RIGHT OF REPLACEMENT OR REFUND - If you discover a defect in this electronic work within 90 days of receiving it, you can receive a refund of the money (if any) you paid for it by sending a written explanation to the person you received the work from. If you received the work on a physical medium, you must return the medium with your written explanation. The person or entity that provided you with the defective work may elect to provide a replacement copy in lieu of a refund. If you received the work electronically, the person or entity providing it to you may choose to give you a second opportunity to receive the work electronically in lieu of a refund. If the second copy is also defective, you may demand a refund in writing without further opportunities to fix the problem.

1.F.4. Except for the limited right of replacement or refund set forth in paragraph 1.F.3, this work is provided to you 'AS-IS', WITH NO OTHER WARRANTIES OF ANY KIND, EXPRESS OR IMPLIED, INCLUDING BUT NOT LIMITED TO WARRANTIES OF MERCHANTIBILITY OR FITNESS FOR ANY PURPOSE.

1.F.5. Some states do not allow disclaimers of certain implied warranties or the exclusion or limitation of certain types of damages. If any disclaimer or limitation set forth in this agreement violates the law of the state applicable to this agreement, the agreement shall be interpreted to make the maximum disclaimer or limitation permitted by the applicable state law. The invalidity or unenforceability of any provision of this agreement shall not void the remaining provisions.

1.F.6. INDEMNITY

- You agree to indemnify and hold the Foundation, the trademark owner, any agent or employee of the Foundation, anyone providing copies of Project Gutenberg-tm electronic works in accordance with this agreement, and any volunteers associated with the production, promotion and distribution of Project Gutenberg-tm electronic works, harmless from all liability, costs and expenses, including legal fees, that arise directly or indirectly from any of the following which you do or cause to occur: (a) distribution of this or any Project Gutenberg-tm work, (b) alteration, modification, or additions or deletions to any Project Gutenberg-tm work, and (c) any Defect you cause.

Section 2. Information about the Mission of Project Gutenberg-tm

Project Gutenberg-tm is synonymous with the free distribution of electronic works in formats readable by the widest variety of computers including obsolete, old, middle-aged and new computers. It exists because of the efforts of hundreds of volunteers and donations from people in all walks of life.

Volunteers and financial support to provide volunteers with the assistance they need, is critical to reaching Project Gutenberg-tm's goals and ensuring that the Project Gutenberg-tm collection will remain freely available for generations to come. In 2001, the Project Gutenberg Literary Archive Foundation was created to provide a secure and permanent future for Project Gutenberg-tm and future generations. To learn more about the Project Gutenberg Literary Archive Foundation and how your efforts and donations can help, see Sections 3 and 4 and the Foundation web page at http://www.gutenberg.net/fundraising/pglaf.

Section 3. Information about the Project Gutenberg Literary Archive Foundation

The Project Gutenberg Literary Archive Foundation is a non profit 501(c)(3) educational corporation organized under the laws of the state of Mississippi and granted tax exempt status by the Internal Revenue Service. The Foundation's EIN or federal tax identification number is 64-6221541. Contributions to the Project Gutenberg Literary Archive Foundation are tax deductible to the full extent permitted by U.S. federal laws and your state's laws.

The Foundation's principal office is located at 4557 Melan Dr. S. Fairbanks, AK, 99712., but its volunteers and employees are scattered throughout numerous locations. Its business office is located at 809 North 1500 West, Salt Lake City, UT 84116, (801) 596-1887, email business@pglaf.org. Email contact links and up to date contact information can be found at the Foundation's web site and official page at http://www.gutenberg.net/about/contact

For additional contact information: Dr. Gregory B. Newby Chief Executive and Director gbnewby@pglaf.org

Section 4. Information about Donations to the Project Gutenberg Literary Archive Foundation

Project Gutenberg-tm depends upon and cannot survive without wide spread public support and donations to carry out its mission of increasing the number of public domain and licensed works that can be freely distributed in machine readable form accessible by the widest array of equipment including outdated equipment. Many small donations ($1 to $5,000) are particularly important to maintaining tax exempt status with the IRS.

The Foundation is committed to complying with the laws regulating charities and charitable donations in all 50 states of the United States. Compliance requirements are not uniform and it takes a considerable effort, much paperwork and many fees to meet and keep up with these requirements. We do not solicit donations in locations where we have not received written confirmation of compliance. To SEND DONATIONS or determine the status of compliance for any particular state visit http://www.gutenberg.net/fundraising/donate

While we cannot and do not solicit contributions from states where we have not met the solicitation requirements, we know of no prohibition against accepting unsolicited donations from donors in such states who approach us with offers to donate.

International donations are gratefully accepted, but we cannot make any statements concerning tax treatment of donations received from outside the United States. U.S. laws alone swamp our small staff.

Please check the Project Gutenberg Web pages for current donation methods and addresses. Donations are accepted in a number of other ways including including checks, online payments and credit card donations. To donate, please visit: http://www.gutenberg.net/fundraising/donate

Section 5. General Information About Project Gutenberg-tm electronic works.

Professor Michael S. Hart is the originator of the Project Gutenberg-tm concept of a library of electronic works that could be freely shared with anyone. For thirty years, he produced and distributed Project Gutenberg-tm eBooks with only a loose network of volunteer support.

Project Gutenberg-tm eBooks are often created from several printed editions, all of which are confirmed as Public Domain in the U.S. unless a copyright notice is included. Thus, we do not necessarily keep eBooks in compliance with any particular paper edition.

Most people start at our Web site which has the main PG search facility:

http://www.gutenberg.net

This Web site includes information about Project Gutenberg-tm, including how to make donations to the Project Gutenberg Literary Archive Foundation, how to help produce our new eBooks, and how to subscribe to our email newsletter to hear about new eBooks.

A Collection of Stories

A free ebook from http://manybooks.net/

Printed in Great Britain
by Amazon